THIS IS TEMPORARY /
HOW TRANSIENT PROJECTS ARE
REDEFINING ARCHITECTURE

EDITED BY:
CATE ST HILL

RIBA ⚏ **Publishing**

© RIBA Enterprises Ltd, 2016

Published by RIBA Publishing, part of RIBA Enterprises Ltd, The Old Post Office, St Nicholas Street, Newcastle upon Tyne, NE1 1RH

ISBN 978 1 85946 606 3

Stock code 85147

The right of Cate St Hill to be identified as the Author of this Work has been asserted in accordance with the Copyright, Designs and Patents Act 1988 sections 77 and 78.

British Library Cataloguing-in-Publication Data
A catalogue record for this book is available from the British Library.

Commissioning editor: Sarah Busby
Production: Michèle Woodger
Designed and typeset by Michèle Woodger
Printed and bound by Pureprint Group, UK
Cover image: © Ben Quinton

While every effort has been made to check the accuracy and quality of the information given in this publication, neither the Author nor the Publisher accept any responsibility for the subsequent use of this information, for any errors or omissions that it may contain, or for any misunderstandings arising from it.

RIBA Publishing is part of RIBA Enterprises Ltd.
www.ribaenterprises.com

ACKNOWLEDGEMENTS

I would like to thank the following people for their invaluable time, patience, inspiration, education and encouragement, without which this book would not have been made possible, in no particular order:

The RIBA, Shumi Bose, Mariana Pestana, Cany Ash, Sam Jacob, Adrian Forty, Murray Fraser, the Bartlett, David Benjamin, Jorge Godoy, Lene Nettelbeck, David Chambers, Kevin Haley, Nicholas Lobo Brennan, Maria Smith, Eddie Blake, Folke Köbberling, Martin Kaltwasser, Lettice Drake, Paloma Gormley, Amica Dall, Jane Hall, Morag Myerscough, Suzanne O'Connell, Xavi Llarch Font, Carolina Caicedo, Holly Lewis, Marco Canevacci, Nicolas Henninger, Olivier Legris and Hiliary St Hill.

/ Cate St Hill, 2015

CONTENTS

ABOUT THE EDITOR AND CONTRIBUTING AUTHORS

Cate St Hill is an architecture and design writer, currently writing for the bi-monthly publication *Blueprint*, and previously for *Building Design*. She has also worked at the British Council and as a researcher for FAT Architecture and Crimson Architectural Historians British Pavilion for the Venice Architecture Biennale in 2014. Cate completed her Part 1 at the Bartlett School of Architecture, before working for a couple of years in practice and receiving a master's in Architectural History, also from the Bartlett. Cate currently lives in London and has a popular self-titled design and architecture blog: **catesthill.com**. This is her first book.

Cany Ash graduated from Cambridge and the University of Westminster. She worked in London, Berlin and New York before founding Ash Sakula Architects with Robert Sakula in 1994. Ash Sakula has established a reputation for working in unpromising sites and creating strong identities for places with mixed public and private clients. The practice is passionate about the intelligent reuse of existing space, passive technologies and innovative construction.

Mariana Pestana is a Portuguese architect and curator. She lives and works in London, where she co-founded the collective The Decorators. Mariana lectured in spatial design at Central Saint Martins and Chelsea College of Arts, and is developing a PhD at the Bartlett School of Architecture. She currently works as a curator at the Victoria and Albert Museum.

Shumi Bose is a London-based writer, editor and teacher. She teaches architectural history and theory at Central Saint Martins and at the Architectural Association. She is a contributing editor at *Blueprint* magazine, also writing for *The Architectural Review*, *PIN-UP* and *Domus*. In 2012, Shumi worked curatorially alongside David Chipperfield on the 13th Venice Biennale of Architecture. She is particularly interested in the relationship between architecture and financial speculation.

FOREWORD

In 1520 Henry VIII travelled to Calais to meet his French counterpart, Francis I - two powerful Renaissance kings desperately trying to out-do each other. How did Henry choose to impress his rival? With temporary architecture. He built a 10,000 square metre palace of 'great and mighty masonry' in four blocks with a central courtyard; each side 100 metres long. Above the brickwork, walls made of fabric and timber frames were painted to look like stone or brick. Cate St Hill's definition of temporary architecture as 'purposely short-lived structures…that create experimental sites for interaction and engagement' confirms that it's nothing new. We've known for centuries that the temporary has so much potential for influencing the permanent – in Henry's case, peace with France.

As a developer deeply interested in creating economically and socially sustainable places, my overriding interest in the temporary is what it can teach me about what to build for the long term. To understand what communities need we must understand people's lives, what motivates them and what makes them happy. The answers come from talking. And listening. And that, for me, is where temporary architecture comes into its own - as a tool for communication, a tool to inspire people to imagine something different, somewhere…else. Beautiful, smaller interventions like Studio Weave's Lullaby Factory or larger, operational facilities like EXYZT's Southwark Lido, designed, built and operated by a team who lived on site while it was open, all serve the same purpose - to challenge our perceptions of place, to open our minds, to ask us questions about how we want to live and, crucially, to delight and surprise. My own work creating temporary interventions with Morag Myerscough has been extraordinarily powerful. It helped us connect with local communities, inspired our architects and planners to design appropriate, site specific schemes and taught us about the places and the people who will use what we build.

As I turned the pages of this wonderful book I felt such a sense of joy at the sheer exuberance exhibited by each and every one of the projects, their bravery and the (probable) lack of funds that delivered them. The people featured in this book are making our towns and cities more beautiful. But it's more than that. They are helping us to understand ourselves better.

/ Martyn Evans, 2015

INTRODUCTION /
CATE ST HILL

Temporary architecture has been getting a bit of stick in recent years. It's often been misrepresented as a flimsy trend, fuelled by a frenzy of meanwhile projects following downturns in construction inactivity and developers cashing in to avoid longer-term problems and difficult questions. It's been seen as a photo-ready quick fix: easy, entertaining, and often, mistakenly, cheap – a marketing ploy to attract investment in an area and show the world it's 'hip'. It is now synonymous with shipping containers, street food and music festivals, and that advertising buzzword 'pop-up'. But there is a long history, continuing today, of a more holistic temporary architecture that deals with fundamental questions of how we might live, work and play more harmoniously together. These structures, situations and events quickly appear and disappear but they are designed to invest and embed themselves in a community, public space or set of ideas. They open up possibilities, test scenarios and subvert preconceptions of what our cities should be like and how we should behave in them. Their architects and designers, often young, are pushing the boundaries of architecture and taking the city back into their own hands.

So, what can we define as temporary architecture? And is it anything new? Temporary architecture in the context of this book can be labelled as purposely short-lived structures, exhibitions and programmes that create experimental sites for interaction and engagement, ranging from a tiny travelling theatre and floating cinema to a community lido on an abandoned railway site and a theatre made entirely from scrap material. Sometimes they are designed for specific biennales, festivals and commissions, but they can also be self-initiated, do-it-yourself building and grass-roots platforms for collective, participatory design. Usually they're experimental and innovative, questioning the form of permanent architecture gone before. Always they're for public use and involve the public as key protagonists in their formation and performance.

If we take temporary architecture to be something that is not permanent, then it has been around, in one form or another, since time immemorial, from prehistoric wooden huts and shelters, through medieval stage sets, circuses and world fairs, to the mobile home and post-war prefabs, and wartime and disaster relief. In contemporary architecture we are more familiar with temporary exhibitions and pavilions: Le Corbusier and Pierre Jeanneret's L'Esprit Nouveau Pavilion (1925), Mies van der Rohe's Barcelona Pavilion (1929), Alison and Peter Smithson's House of the Future for the Daily Mail Ideal Home Exhibition in London (1956) and Charles and Ray Eames' IBM Pavilion at the New York World's Fair (1964-65) – prototypes for modern living that showed their creators' provocative ideas on the future of architecture and urbanism. They were also about transforming architectural forms into compelling, memorable visual images – a form of advertisement. Archigram also challenged conventional approaches with mobile, inflatable or temporary components, pods and capsules in the 1960s and 1970s, with projects that embraced the digital information revolution including Walking City, Plug-in City and Instant City (although these remained unbuilt). The Smithsons, however, saw temporary architecture as following in the tradition of the centuries-old theatrical structures that defined tastes and trends:[1]

"The architects of the Renaissance established ways of going about things which perhaps we unconsciously follow: for example, between the idea sketchily stated and the commission for the permanent building came the stage-architecture of the court masque; the architectural settings and decorations for the birthday of the prince, for the wedding of a ducal daughter, for the entry of a Pope into a city state; these events were used as opportunities for the realisation of the new style; the new sort of space; the new weight of decoration; made real perhaps for a single day… the transient enjoyably consumed, creating the taste for the permanent."[2]

These concepts and ideas about rethinking society, seen in these pavilions, are similar in many ways to the temporary structures featured in this book – building 'alternative possible worlds', not entirely real, not entirely fictional, as The Decorators' Mariana Pestana notes in her essay on page 141. Yet the architecture here is also somehow different: they're not prescribing or dictating specific ways to live in the future; nor are they prototypes to be repeated on a grander scale. Instead, each is a unique (and sometimes bizarre), rule-breaking structure, a vehicle for playing with thoughts and ideas – and it is these thoughts and ideas, and often not the physical thing itself, that could have an impact on the future of architecture. It's also more about the process of building and the political nature of architecture, as we shall find out.

This book features 13 interviews with 13 architects and designers, ranging widely from the more traditional small architecture practices and studios to multidisciplinary collectives and cross-discipline designers, spread across the world from New York and Santiago to London, Berlin and Zürich. All have started their own firms and continue to work on their own terms. Each has, in his or her own way, inspired new definitions of architecture, not just in terms of their physical outcomes, but also in the way that they go about creating them – and that's why they've been singled out here. I have tried to avoid some better-known, medium-sized practices that also do temporary architecture, mainly because I wanted to include smaller, younger architects and designers that are collectively 'emerging' as a sort of new generation of subversive, socially minded practices.

What they all have in common, apart from being relatively young in architectural terms and infectiously passionate about their craft, is a concern for engaging people and enriching local communities, and for collaborative, participatory ways of designing, making and building. These architects aren't daydreamers: they're making extraordinary things happen. The projects here are inventive, experimental and playful, but at the same time they're also well-considered and empowering ways to create animated, deeply rooted places in the neglected, disused and sometimes inaccessible parts of our cities. The book is divided into six themes or features: Young architects' programmes; Public realm and engagement; Playful storytellers; Collectives and self-initiated projects; Participative building and materiality; and The art world and temporary architecture. It is organised so that each chapter represents two or three practices that exemplify one of these features. Many of the practices' work crosses over these themes and the placing of a particular practice within one chapter rather than another is purely for the purposes of drawing out similarities and connections between groups, and organising the content into a cohesive whole.

These 13 architects are just a fraction of the whole picture; they are not meant to comprise an exhaustive list but to illustrate the temporary architecture phenomenon today. They are largely confined to urban areas, most predominately big cities such as London, Paris, Berlin and New York, but that is not to say that temporary architecture is not happening in more peripheral situations or rural locations. If a study were to be done of all the little temporary installations, events and exhibitions taking place across the world, by architects and laymen alike, the list could go on indefinitely. This book is simply a succinct representation of the temporary situation in this moment in time.

The first chapter deals with young architects' programmes, namely the MoMA PS1 Young Architects Program, an inspiring annual competition open to emerging architects and students that requires them to design a temporary structure for the summer on a site in Long Island City, New York. It has since expanded to similar initiatives across the world in Rome, Santiago, Istanbul and Seoul. The programme allows young architects the freedom and support to test out ideas, experiment with innovative structural approaches and materials, and put their previously unrealised methods into practice. This chapter aims to show how programmes like these are creating unique opportunities for small, young practices with limited previous built experience, such as New York-based The Living and Chilean-German practice GUN Architects, and how they can be formative to those practices developing their own manifesto.

Chapter 2 looks at architecture practices that are creating public realm projects, urban studies and area strategies in order to develop a deeper understanding of an urban area and to engage local communities in long-term change. This chapter includes London-based We Made That and multidisciplinary team The Decorators (made up of an architect, an interior designer, a psychologist and a landscape architect). Both practices have developed creative, tailor-made programmes for neglected, run-down high streets and sites across London, from Poplar's Chrisp Street Market to Croydon's restaurant district. Initiatives include a radio station for broadcasting debates, an online town team to help crowd-source ideas and a toolkit to help communities create their own temporary and meanwhile projects in empty shops and vacant land. This chapter aims to show how temporary architecture isn't purely concerned with temporary structures, but can comprise a whole host of initiatives – a complicated sum of vibrant parts. Similarly, but perhaps a bit more playfully, the third chapter focuses on imaginative, young practices creating temporary structures backed up by rigorous research into the history of a place and the construction of whimsical narratives. Profiled are Studio Weave and Aberrant Architecture, who both share deep social aspirations to connect these physical structures with people and place.

The fourth theme centres on multidisciplinary collectives who are pioneering a self-initiated style of building that engages local communities in the making process, and relies on collaborative, hands-on teamwork. Here, we meet French collective EXYZT, a motley team of architects, artists, graphic designers and photographers that completely inhabit a project for the few weeks or months that it is around, as well as London-based Assemble and Practice Architecture, who were both influenced by working with EXYZT on Southwark Lido in 2008. All three groups are redefining the scope of conventional architectural education and practice, showing how post-recession young architects can forge their own path and have a profound impact on our cities. Taking this idea further, Chapter 5 looks at two Berlin-based teams also challenging preceding traditions: artist-duo Folke Köbberling and Martin Kaltwasser, and Plastique Fantastique. Both use materials to gather and empower people to think about sustainable, self-initiated acts of building.

The final chapter deals with the blurring lines between disciplines, namely the art world and the architecture world, in the creation of temporary architecture. Case studies here include Zürich-based GRUPPE and London-based Morag Myerscough, who trained in graphic design but has since gone on to collaborate with architects and developers on temporary pavilions, installations and wayfinding projects. This chapter aims to illustrate how temporary architecture can slip between disciplines, none superior to any other. Instead, it's about opening up creative possibilities, expanding design processes and embracing collaboration – architecture as a cultural movement.

All the chapters attempt to depict alternative modes of practising architecture that go slightly against the norm and challenge the conventional role of the architect. In this book, I hope to show that although only around for a short amount of time, these temporary projects can, for an intense moment, provide shared, valuable experiences in urban public spaces. They are not just about appearance, but about the evolution of ideas and processes. Finally, I hope to show that temporary architecture is more than just a trend – rather, it is a sustainable model of building for the future.

CHAPTER 01 /
YOUNG ARCHITECTS' PROGRAMMES: TESTING, TESTING, TESTING

INTERVIEWS:
THE LIVING [USA] / GUN ARCHITECTS [CHILE]

Not many architectural competitions or commissions are open exclusively to young architects or small practices – they are few and far between. The UK's annual Serpentine Pavilion, a commission to create a temporary structure on the lawn of the Serpentine Galleries in London, is increasingly inviting younger, lesser-known talent such as Madrid-based selgascano and Chilean Smiljan Radic, but even then, young in architectural terms can mean a practice with several years' experience and a director with an average age of 40. There are some exceptions, though, and it's often contemporary art galleries that are paving the way, fusing art and architecture practices to curate pop-up events, temporary installations and residencies.

Hauser & Wirth, for instance, launched a competition – part of its architecture season in spring 2015 – called The Shed Project, inviting recent architecture graduates (applicants had to be under 35 and to be studying for, or have recently completed, RIBA Part 3 Architecture) to design an out-building for an artist residency programme at its new rural Somerset outpost.

Initiatives such as these allow young practitioners and practices to test out ideas in the supportive environment of well-established art institutions – institutions that enjoy the open-mindedness of the art world rather than the rules and regulations of the architecture world. One such example is the hugely successful MoMA PS1 Young Architects Program (YAP), a veritable laboratory for experimentation and innovation that requires its participants to employ a creative use of time, resources and space. YAP is an annual competition which gives emerging architects the opportunity to build a temporary structure on a large triangular concrete courtyard in Long Island City, Queens, New York. Inaugurated in 2000, the programme was formed primarily to solidify the affiliation between The Museum of Modern Art in Manhattan and MoMA PS1 (formerly P.S.1), an art institution founded in 1971 by Alanna Heiss with the mission of turning abandoned buildings in New York City into artist studios and exhibition spaces.

The aim of the YAP was initially to simply provide a partially shaded outdoor space for visitors and the local community for the summer – a place to stop and pause amidst the hustle and bustle of New York's all-consuming, densely packed urban environment. Over the years since, the programme has become an outlet for young, energetic talent to experiment with a wide spectrum of inventive structural approaches and materials, from bamboo and cardboard tubes to air-cleaning particles and biodegradable bricks, and for many, it's their first formative experience of designing, fundraising and constructing a real, tangible, built form.

For these young architects it's an opportunity to manifest the ideas and concepts that have often previously been confined to paper architecture or university crit rooms. Suddenly they're dealing with a very public, very complicated urban space, sandwiched between a busy avenue and the home of MoMA PS1, a red-brick Romanesque Revival building, with views of Manhattan's skyscrapers on the horizon. Here, they can play with and manipulate issues ranging from public engagement and interaction, to shelter and occupation of an urban space, freed from some of the rules and regulations that constrain more traditional, permanent projects.

Moreover, there is the spotlight that the MoMA casts – a worldwide stage, a tremendous opportunity. In many ways it's the dream project for practices first starting out, wishing to bridge the gap between the theories of university and real-life practice. Winner of the 2014 structure, The Living co-founder, David Benjamin, interviewed over the next few pages, sees the programme as a platform for ideas: 'It's a really unique programme, especially in the United States – it's just so optimistic about the future. One of the things it does is give young firms the opportunity to actually develop and build something

FIGURE 1.1: previous / Water Cathedral by GUN Architects was inspired by the dry weather of Santiago and responded to the theme of water

FIGURE 1.2: opposite / the Hi-Fy structure hosted Warm Up, an experimental concert series now in its 18th year

out in public. That chance alone, I think, is very rare and very useful.' For Lene Nettelbeck, one half of GUN Architects, also interviewed, who created a structure for Chile's version YAP_CONSTRUCTO in 2011, the programme offers the opportunity for connection and immediate feedback from the public getting in direct contact with the structures: the programme is 'outside of university or academic research, meaning that the general public [can] access it and evaluate it and experience it'. It's that experiential element that is perhaps the most exciting for these architects – the opportunity to create a space for interaction and participation.

Architects of the programme are also required to address environmental issues, such as sustainability and recycling – in 2012, HWKN's bright blue scaffold made of nylon fabric was sprayed with titania nanoparticles to clean the air (said to be the equivalent of taking 260 cars off the road), while The Living's Hy-Fi (see page 15) from 2014 created almost no waste and no carbon emissions. For that project The Living invented a lightweight, biodegradable brick – made of chopped up corn stalks and a living organism called mycelium – to form a 12m-high circular tower. At the end of the two-month period, the structure was taken apart and the bricks composted, returning the physical materials to the earth in an estimated 60 days. 'This project is no small feat,' notes Pedro Gadanho, curator at MoMA's department of architecture and design. 'Referring to the latest developments in biotech, it reinvents the most basic component of architecture – the brick – as both a material of the future and a classic trigger for open-ended design possibilities.' The project, being only around for a short amount of time, raised serious, unavoidable questions about the profession's use of materials as well as lifecycles in construction. Says The Living co-founder David Benjamin: 'In our temporary projects, we mean to point to bigger possibilities for the way we make buildings. With our idea of compostable building blocks, it's not only about one example of a new building material, it's an approach to thinking about material selection. It could mean recycling or reusing some of the building components so we can minimise the amount we're just throwing into the landfill.'

The MoMA PS1 programme has since expanded internationally to Zaha Hadid's MAXXI building in Rome, Italy (since 2011), CONSTRUCTO in Santiago, Chile (since 2010; first opened to just Chilean architects, later expanded to Latin America), Istanbul Museum of Modern Art in Turkey (since 2013, and now every two years) and the National Museum of Modern and Contemporary Art in Seoul, Korea (since 2014). In each iteration, it continues the original aim of providing opportunities for talented young designers to create a space for live summer events in public squares or courtyards. Notable projects include SO? Architecture and Ideas' subtly shifting landscape of mirrored discs that floated on the hidden waterline of the Bosphorus next to Istanbul Modern, and Seoul's first installation, Shinseon Play by Moon Ji Bang, where visitors could jump on trampolines through a cluster of cloud-like balloons that gently swayed in response to pre-programmed changes in air pressure.

FIGURE 1.3: opposite / the Rainforest Pavilion was based on the dripping structure of the Water Cathedral in Chile, created by GUN Architects at the Architectural Association in London in 2014

THIS IS TEMPORARY

Santiago-based GUN Architects, interviewed on page 25, created Water Cathedral, the second structure for YAP_CONSTRUCTO in Chile. Slender, vertical components hung or rose up like stalactites and stalagmites in a cave, varying in height and density to provide shelter and shade. Water, fed by a hydraulic irrigation system, dripped from these hanging elements to cool down visitors. This was GUN's first public project, a major step that led first to their nomination for the Emerging Architecture awards organised by London's *Architectural Review* and eventually to their constructing a replica structure for the Architectural Association. 'That situation really changed the whole office concept fundamentally because it was the first chance to put our methods into practice,' muses co-founder Jorge Godoy in our interview. 'It was also kind of an intervention into thinking about the Chilean context, turning around the thinking that it wouldn't be possible because there's no culture of installations of temporary buildings here. Without the MoMA programme, no way could we have done something similar.'

Rather than necessarily leading to bigger projects or instant recognition (though sometimes they do), for many the concepts and ideas explored in the MoMA PS1 programme sow the seeds for future projects, and help define and focus the practice's voice. 'Since Liquid Sky, we continue to think about the nature of temporary, installation architecture,' says Los Angeles-based Ball-Nogues, who created its structure in 2007. 'We believe this is very important to consider – YAP projects have short lives. We are skeptical of the view of YAP as a kind of surrogate, or an exercise for young architects who will one day start making "real" buildings. We continue to explore temporality in our practice while viewing impermanent environments as potentially rich experiential moments in public space and investigations into the physicality of building.'

The Living also uses elements of its research into Hy-Fi to inform its 'low-tech biotech' approach – combining biological technologies and cutting-edge engineering to create new building materials, foster environmental awareness and prototype the architecture of the future. One of the experimental approaches the practice has developed during its ongoing research has been coined 'flash research' – inventing projects that have self-imposed constraints, such as a budget of less than $1,000 or a duration of three months or less, in order to experiment with new ideas. One outcome is Living Glass, a thin transparent membrane that 'breathes' in response to sensors. Concludes Benjamin: 'I do think that these temporary projects have a really unique role. Despite being small, and despite being temporary, and for most of them despite having a low budget, they really point to new possibilities for architecture that could have a huge impact on the way many other buildings are designed and made.'

In the interviews over the following pages, however, both The Living and GUN Architects agree that there could be more programmes like the MoMA PS1 and, ultimately, that the profession is not doing enough to foster this type of architecture, particularly in regards to opportunities for younger firms. It is a frustration felt across the world. In 2013, for example, an RIBA Business Benchmarking Report of every chartered practice in the UK revealed an increasing gulf between the smallest and largest practices. It found that 40% of British Architects are employed by just 3% of practices, and that the majority of firms employ fewer than six staff. It means that it is increasingly difficult for small practices to grow and win increasingly bigger projects. The Living and GUN Architects suggest that the city itself could do more, whether by private and public organisations engaging more with temporary urban interventions, supporting young architects financially with funding for projects, or by involving small practices in more permanent public and civic projects in the city.

Initiatives such as the MoMA PS1 give young architects the space to challenge their curiosity and creativity in an intense period of time. What would ordinarily be developed piecemeal over a period of years, on the side of smaller architectural jobs, unwon competition entries and teaching, is condensed into a small, powerful structure. Yet, while there is a need for more programmes like YAP in the profession, it is architectural education that could also learn the most from this way of working – by creating real, built projects that inspire innovation and test out ideas.

INTERVIEW 01 /
THE LIVING

DAVID BENJAMIN

The Living is a New York-based practice set up by David Benjamin and Soo-in Yang in 2006 with the mission of 'exploring the architecture of the future through building it today'. With an interest in new technologies, design innovation and sustainability, it believes cities and buildings are living, breathing organisms and has a passion for the way that targeted constructions can activate 'urban organisms'. Clients include the City of New York, Airbus, 3M, Quantified Self and Miami Science Museum. Recent projects include the Princeton Architecture Laboratory for research on robotics and next-generation design and construction technologies and Pier 35 EcoPark, a 60m-long floating pier in the East River of New York that changes colour according to water quality. David Benjamin is also assistant professor at Columbia University Graduate School of Architecture, Planning and Preservation.

Cate St Hill: What attracted you to the MoMA PS1 programme?

David Benjamin: The competition has been on my radar for many years and I have always admired it for giving young architecture firms a platform to experiment with a new architectural idea or approach. I think it's a really unique programme, especially in the United States – it's just so optimistic about the future. It has a great legacy: there are so many firms that have won the competition in the past and made really interesting installations in the courtyard of MoMA PS1, and have then gone on to do some really amazing work that in many cases is built up from their initial explorations there.

The process is pretty interesting – it's a two-stage competition. The first stage involves a number of different young firms being nominated and asked to submit a portfolio of past work. We were nominated in 2013, then we were one of five firms selected to go into the next round and create a proposal for the courtyard in 2014.

What was the concept for your proposal, Hy-Fi?

DB: The idea was to explore a new approach to materials and lifecycles in architecture and construction. More specifically, we were interested in using materials with low embodied energy and creating an installation that would be, in many ways, a design that disappeared as much as appeared. In the United States, as in many parts of the world, up to 40% of our landfill is made of construction waste – this is a huge material problem. If we could have other options for

FIGURE 1.4: previous / Hy-Fi stood for two months in the courtyard of MoMA PS1 in Long Island City, Queens, New York
FIGURE 1.5: above / it was part of the MoMA PS1 Young Architects Program in 2014

architectural materials and other approaches to making our buildings, I think it could be really helpful and interesting.

In order to play out the big idea, we worked on developing a new building material – a biodegradable brick. It's basically made from agricultural waste, such as chopped up corn stalks, combined with a living organism called mycelium, which is the root-like structure of mushrooms. When you combine these two simple, organic ingredients and put them into a mould of any shape, in about five days it grows together and solidifies into a solid object. This allowed us to create a very lightweight, very low-cost, biodegradable brick, with almost no waste, almost no energy required and almost no carbon emissions. We used 10,000 of these bricks to create a 12m-high structure in the courtyard of

MoMA PS1. At the end of the project, we took the structure apart and composted all of the bricks.

To summarise, most architectural projects approach the natural environment by taking high value raw materials, using a lot of energy to convert them into building blocks, and, at the end of the useful life of a building, the material ends up in landfill. In contrast, we took low value raw materials, we spent no energy converting them into building blocks, and then we returned that physical material to the earth in about 60 days instead of hundreds or even thousands of years.

FIGURE 1.6: above / Hi-Fy was a 12m-high circular tower made from biodegradable bricks

FIGURE 1.7: above /10,000 bricks were used to create the tower in the courtyard of MoMA PS1

What was the reaction to Hy-Fi once it had been built and installed in the MoMA PS1 courtyard?

DB: I think it was really interesting to see the spectrum of reactions. For one, the project has won a Holcim Award for sustainability, so within the discussion of sustainable architecture, with this international competition and an international jury, the project was validated as an interesting concept and design. At the same time, there was a huge amount of interest from the general public and even the popular media. That was really interesting to see too, because people really understood the simple idea of making a building that is compostable. People were very interested in that idea.

Do you think the MoMA PS1 programme puts young architects on the map? Do you think it has the ability to help practices in the longer term?

DB: I think it definitely does. One of the things it does is give young firms the opportunity to actually develop and build something out in public. That chance alone I think is very rare and very useful. It's such a great opportunity for any young firm. But in addition to that, MoMA and MoMA PS1 have brought this great thing to the project, which is their network — anything that MoMA does gets a lot of attention, so it's just such a great way for a firm and a project to have a public platform for their ideas. We really found that to be true, it was really exciting — it was such an honour.

FIGURE 1.8: above / one of the biodegradable bricks, made of chopped up corn stalks and a living organism called mycelium

Do you think there are enough opportunities like the MoMA PS1 programme for young architecture practices? Is the profession doing enough to foster this type of architecture?

DB: I think there should be more programmes like this or ones that are related in their aim, but that might give other opportunities to young firms. For example, if there could be some way to allow and encourage young firms to compete in design competitions for small, public projects in the city, such as libraries or public schools, I think that would be of great benefit to both the young firms and the architectural culture, but also to the public and the city. I don't think the city would suffer in any way from doing this, I don't think it would be a big risk, but it would be a huge pay-off.

Were there any precedents in your past work for Hy-Fi?

DB: We had done some other temporary projects, like a project a few years ago called Amphibious Architecture, which involved bringing the Internet of Things out into the public. More specifically, it placed a floating network of six-foot long tubes in the East River that had sensors below water and lights above water. The sensors detected things like water quality, presence of fish, human interest in environmental issues, then the lights changed colour and blinked according to the data. It was basically a way of making a public interface to the river ecosystem, so this cloud of light changed colour and blinked to make visible the invisible. It was a totally different concept for us than the PS1 project, but similarly it was a small installation that pointed to a

FIGURE 1.9: above / Amphibious Architecture placed a floating network of six-foot long tubes in the East River of New York, with sensors that monitored water quality, presence of fish and human interest in the river ecosystem, 2010

much larger idea. The larger idea, really, in the Amphibious Architecture project was to imagine that the building façades of the city and the skyline of the city, including the water, could come alive and have a layer of information that was valuable and relevant to the public.

Do you think these temporary projects can bring something more meaningful to an area or community than their original size or budget would initially suggest?

DB: I do think that these temporary projects have a really unique role. Despite being small, and despite being temporary, and for most of them despite having a low budget, they really point to new possibilities for architecture that could be much more widespread and could have a huge impact on the way many other buildings are designed and made. For example, with our idea of compostable building blocks, it's not only about one example of a new building material, it's an approach to thinking about materials selection and maybe allowing that there are new and better ways to make construction materials that could be relevant to many different projects and permanent buildings.

This doesn't necessarily mean putting mycelium in buildings, it could mean choosing mineral wool as insulation instead of extruded styrofoam, or it could mean recycling or reusing some of the building components so we can minimise the amount we're just throwing into landfill. So, in our temporary projects, we mean to point to bigger possibilities for the way we make buildings.

FIGURE 1.10: above / lights changed colour and blinked according to the data collected by the sensors underwater

What ambitions do you have for your practice over the next five or 10 years? Do you think you will continue to create temporary projects or develop similar ideas?

DB: Yes, in a number of ways. We aim to continue doing projects like the one for MoMA PS1 where we are experimenting with a new idea and pushing some new possibilities. In addition, we would like to take some of the ideas that we have worked with and use them in some of our own more traditional, more permanent buildings. For example, we're currently designing a small laboratory building for Princeton University. It will be a permanent building – it's not so experimental, it's not temporary – but one of the things we are doing is using materials that have extremely low embodied energy. The building will be rated LEED Gold, but on top of that we will be using some of the techniques we experimented with in Hy-Fi. We'd like to continue working in that way, using small insights from our experimental projects to form part of our more mainstream architecture.

FIGURE 1.11: opposite / crowds flocked to MoMA PS1 in the hot summer months of 2014
FIGURE 1.12: above / the Hy-Fi tower was formed of a lightweight biodegradable brick invented by The Living

INTERVIEW 02 /
GUN ARCHITECTS

LENE NETTELBECK
/ JORGE GODOY

GUN Architects is a German-Chilean office founded by architects Lene Nettelbeck and Jorge Godoy. Settled in Santiago, Chile since 2010, GUN engages in architectural and urban projects that are deeply connected with the local environmental and cultural realities of Chile. Its Water Cathedral Pavilion was the winning entry for YAP_CONSTRUCTO, the Santiago arm of MoMA's PS1 Young Architects Program (for which it was also highly commended in the AR Emerging Architecture award 2012), while it is currently working on a masterplan for a self-sufficient community near the Tongoy Peninsula in Chile.

How and when did you start GUN Architects?

Lene Nettelbeck: GUN has existed since 2010, but it didn't really start as an office. I came to Chile from Germany and it wasn't really clear how long I would stay for; Jorge was teaching and wanted to focus more on practice and take some distance away from academia. Suddenly, we had a small project on our hands and started working from home, but without really formalising anything. That first project was the Naturalist Pavilion; this was really something we just started to model on the kitchen table.

We had to really get involved in the project also as builders because of the budget and the innovative nature of this structure – nobody knew how to weave bamboo bars – so we were there on site testing. In those terms, it was a very spontaneous start to the practice, there was no decision, 'Yes, I'll go to Chile and we'll start an office.'

After that, we were invited to present a proposal for the Young Architects Program International in Chile [YAP_CONSTRUCTO], where we fortunately won the competition. That situation really changed the whole office concept fundamentally because it was the first chance to put our methods into practice, working with other people and developing a large-scale public project. Right now, we are getting more consolidated as a team and have a long-term research agenda in Chile and Germany. Somehow we are more official but it still feels like we're just starting – that's the nice part.

How many of your projects would you consider to be temporary?

Jorge Godoy: Three of our projects can be considered as temporary. The Water Cathedral and Rainforest were both originally designed as temporary structures with a clear duration and standing times on the public space. On the other side, there is the Naturalist Pavilion, a bamboo structure that is gradually disappearing and getting absorbed by nature – a kind of long-term temporary building, where different bits and pieces of the original built structure have started to collapse and to fall apart, getting replaced by the growing plants that interweave with the original structure.

Let's talk about that project, the Naturalist Pavilion. How did the project come about and what was the concept for it?

JG: The Naturalist Pavilion was built just after a huge earthquake we had in 2010, really one of the strongest the country has suffered from in the last 100 years. Many buildings were destroyed and it showed that we have quite serious building deficiencies. In our case, a family farm located close to the epicentre had a garden pavilion fabricated with local traditional materials such as heavy clay roof tiles. The structure couldn't stand the seismic movements and collapsed due to its own weight and rigidity. That situation turned into an opportunity for us to test new materials, lighter and more flexible ones. So we used Chilean bamboo, or caña coligüe, which is quite a good, cheap and novel option that allowed us to create a more elastic woven bamboo structure, where the weaving pattern had all its parts interconnected as a 3D mesh. This monostructure can dynamically respond to seismic movements, absorbing and releasing ground vibrations. The pavilion was built as a series of arches with 2,500 horizontally interwoven bamboo bars ranging in length from 2.5m to 4m. It was a layering system to create a bonded surface, with difference thicknesses and different degrees of permeability for the management of natural light.

Over time, the vegetation that we planted next to the arches also started to weave through them and after two or three years the pavilion started to become run down, just because of natural conditions. It's still standing but what is nice is that the vegetation is getting stronger and thicker; it's taking the shape of the arches. It's interesting to think that at some point the whole pavilion could disappear and the nature would still be standing, completely interwoven. It shows another kind of temporary pavilion that was not planned to be temporary, but ended up as a long-term temporary.

The Water Cathedral in 2011 was part of the Young Architects Program (YAP) in Santiago. Can you tell me a bit more about that project and the process of the programme?

JG: The Water Cathedral came as an invitation. I don't really know how it works in the rest of the world, but in Chile you must be invited to show your work and then you enter the competition with four other offices or architects. There was an international jury, including Barry Bergdoll from the New York MoMA, who chose the winner. Especially here, they wanted to bring back one of the essential points that MoMA PS1 first started to deal with 15 years ago, which was water.

FIGURE 1.13: previous / Water Cathedral featured a canopy of stalactites and stalagmites fed by a hydraulic irrigation system, dripping water onto visitors in need of a cool down in the Valparaíso heat
FIGURE 1.14: above / the textile stalactites of Water Cathedral form a patterned shade on the floor of the pavilion

With our proposal, the Water Cathedral, we wanted to give presence to the water, considering the dry weather in Santiago, especially in the summertime. Conceptually, it also crossed over with some of our previous material research, and with the academic work I did in the north of Chile about fog collection in the desert. Then we took it as a chance to develop it on an urban scale and environment and created a dripping structure. It was a canopy built out of singular textile stalactites that worked as mediators or interfaces between a water network placed over the stalactites and a ground surface populated with a topography of concrete stalagmites below. These stalagmites worked as water collectors, sitting places and a playground for children. The project created the possibility of having different dynamic atmospheres dependent on the length and density of stalactites, changing and shaping different types of spaces and environmental conditions.

So how did that project turn into the Rainforest Pavilion at the Architectural Association in London in 2014?

JG: That's a long story. After we built the Water Cathedral, we got several after-effects, the project was featured in different publications, and we decided at that time to participate in the Emerging Architecture awards organised by *The Architectural Review* in London, at which the Water Cathedral was highly commended. So we went to London for the Awards exhibition opening and gave a lecture to present the project. For us the UK has been an opening space, a platform where we could start to create connections with

FIGURE 1.15: opposite / concrete stalagmites on the floor acted as water collectors, seats and a place for children to play
FIGURE 1.16: above / water collects in one of the Water Cathedral's concrete 'stalagmites'

the Architectural Association and some other people and institutions. I studied at the AA but after I finished I was pretty much detached from it, I had never really come back to the School in the last eight years. We had a meeting with Brett Steele and the exhibition team led by Vanessa Norwood and they all really liked the project. At the beginning it was just going to be a small exhibition, but then Vanessa decided it had to be stronger. She was quite ambitious about it having the atmosphere of the Water Cathedral – the same immersive condition that it had. That was a new challenge for us, in terms of context, fundraising and finding the way to make it.

Something important to mention regarding the project evolution is that the original London version of the Water Cathedral was not really meant to be a pavilion, but a cascade on the front of the school. We worked a long time on that, months actually. It was a beautiful project, really a symbol for the façade – it was going to be a dripping cascade, 15m high, covering 36 Bedford Square. Everything was going fairly well with the engineers and Camden Council in terms of permits, but at the very last minute we got a message from English Heritage saying that the project, however temporary, would cause visual harm to the consistent terrace of late 18th-century, Grade I-listed buildings in Bedford Square.

LN: Even though it was temporary, they were very concerned about Bedford Square, as London's finest and best-preserved Georgian Square. They said that the installation, however interesting as a piece of art in its own right, breaks this visual consistency and draws attention away from the historic buildings. So,

FIGURE 1.17: above /the Rainforest Pavilion viewed from above

we would need to demonstrate public benefits that outweighed the harm, but due to our time frame their advice would be to consider building the installation in Bedford Square as has been traditionally done before.

JG: Even though we were not touching the building at all – we had a full scaffolding system on top of the roof so the façade was completely untouched – English Heritage had a strong concern as well about triggering something that could later be repeated on other buildings in Bedford Square.

LN: That change of direction was very challenging because basically we had to start from scratch, reformulating our design for a new installation that had to stand on the street. It meant new constraints and public regulations,

such as the impossibility of laying anything in terms of foundations in the ground. There was no chance to replicate what the Water Cathedral did in Santiago. However, facing this situation and going for a new installation opened new research paths and positive effects.

JG: The Rainforest for us brought a full new issue in relation to public space. Even though it was built in an area of London that is full of spatial regulations and restrictions, people really accepted and used it. For example, we had a ground of stones and in the beginning there was a lot of fear from the neighbours that their cars were going to be scratched or the windows were going to be destroyed, people were afraid of the textiles burning, or the pond getting full of rubbish, but absolutely nothing like that happened. That opened for us a full new thinking:

FIGURE 1.18: above / visitors scramble over the rocks of the Rainforest Pavilion in London's Bedford Square

FIGURE 1.19: above/unlike the Water Cathedral, the 5m-high Rainforest Pavilion did not have any foundations and was not
allowed to impact the groundwork of Bedford Square

that when you do something that the community accepts and likes, it doesn't get destroyed. Even if we saw some people sleeping there overnight, there was never any kind of violent action against the project. That went against the whole policy of over-safety that is covering London at the moment.

Is it important to you how people engage with the project?

JG: Yes. We had for example one meeting with the Bloomsbury Association (which is related to Bedford Square), who wanted to know who we were. They took to the Rainforest Pavilion quite differently to previous ones. Other pavilions had been much lighter or sculptural, but for them the Rainforest engaged with more environmental and public space dimensions.

LN: It was for them a pavilion they felt you could be part of, because it's not just sculptural, you can go within it. I think that was, for them, the interesting part. It was not just there to be observed – you could use it and experience it as a small new atmosphere in central London.

What happened to the structure afterwards? Did it have an afterlife?

JG: The structure is now stored somewhere out of London in a barn. The scaffolder took the structure. It's still our piece but it's not clear what is going to happen to it.

Going back to the Young Architects Program, do you think you would have been able to do such a project without that initiative?

JG: Definitely not. We were able to build quite a big intervention – it was 700 sq m and had about 3,500 stalactites – and it was also kind of an intervention into thinking about the Chilean context, turning around the thinking that it wouldn't be possible because there's no culture of installations or temporary buildings here. Without the MoMA programme, no way could we have done something similar.

LN: The nice thing about the MoMA programme is that it focuses on young people. There are some pavilions around, but they're from well-known offices, and mainly for fairs or for creating images for companies. This was more experimental, I think. Without this programme I don't know how something like this could happen. Also, it was outside of university life or academic research, meaning that the general public could access it and evaluate it and experience it. That's also something very interesting, it gives you feedback straight away, it's not a workshop you do on a university campus. That's what was nice about working with the AA: the Rainforest Pavilion was within the AA, but it was also part of the city and urban life.

Of course, the programme pushes you in a really very short time to develop it. I think if you make it as a long-term research and it's over years, you have time to find money and make prototypes. I mean, 700 sq m in over five months – it's very big. Also the history of the MoMA PS1 helps you to get interest within the architectural world. It's not something in Santiago, Chile – 'Who cares?' It's part of a very well-known programme. It was, of course, for us, very helpful.

JG: It forces you to be very concrete and pragmatic. It's like one chance to put your ideas in action.

Do you think there should be more programmes like it? Is the profession doing enough to help this type of architecture?

JG: We think definitely there should be more programmes like it. I think it has to do also with some other agents or actors – the city probably has to be much more involved, and private or public institutions should engage more with this issue. Temporary structures or temporary pavilions are not exceptional pieces; they could help generate new ideas for city development or planning.

Architects could be more interested in that and participate more, but if there's not support from higher up and the state, it's basically not possible to go further – money is always a big issue. Even if it's really small, you have to work really hard in order to get something. In our case, the AA, the Chilean Ministry of Culture and the British Council played a fundamental role providing us with not just the money, but also the urban and cultural context for this kind of intervention.

What are you working on at the moment?

LN: We're working on a long-term project that we started three or four years ago. It's located 500km up north from Santiago in a coastal enclave just on the edge of where the desert starts. The main target is to build a self-sufficient community on a territory of 100 ha of post-agricultural land which used to be part of an old

hacienda. As it's a sustainable project, we're not directly connected to any city around; it's an area near to the beach but with a strong rural context. It will start as a cluster of six houses and gradually will increase its urban density, population and infrastructure over the next 20 years.

JG: The project is interesting because it's meant to be something consolidated and long-term, but many of the landscape and infrastructural elements we have to build will be temporary, like small observation platforms, viewpoints or wind towers. They are helping to give an architectural identity to the place supporting the growing process of this development. For us it's the first crossover between managing something that's meant to be a long-term land transformation in a rural urbanisation, with the implementation of iconic and temporary pieces of infrastructure.

What ambitions do you have for the future? Will you continue to work on similar temporary projects?

JG: Yes, we hope to continue our relation with the AA and the British Council – or some other institutions interested in our work – to keep on developing the research that was opened by the Water Cathedral, but slightly reformulated, and producing different outcomes such as the Rainforest, in terms of microclimates, small

atmospheres and this kind of oasis condition. Bedford Square is pretty alive with nature, but it's closed and people cannot really use it; we had the Rainforest outside, and it was beautiful to see how some insects, birds and nature somehow migrated there and inhabited it too without any kind of previous planning. That's a strength of a temporary installation.

FIGURE 1.20: opposite / Rainforest Pavilion was installed during the summer of 2014 outside the Architecture Association
FIGURE 1.21: above top / schematic drawing of the Rainforest Pavilion in the wild
FIGURE 1.22: above bottom / visualisation of the Rainforest Pavilion in Bedford Square, London

CHAPTER 02 /
PUBLIC REALM AND ENGAGEMENT: FACILITATING POSSIBILITIES AND ANIMATING PLACES

INTERVIEWS:
WE MADE THAT [UK] / THE DECORATORS [UK]

Temporary architecture isn't purely pop-ups and pretty pavilions, disappearing as quickly as they appear; it can also be something far subtler, involving a wide range of participants and stakeholders working together with deeper social ambitions for our shared public spaces. Rather than building one particular physical structure, these public realm projects, urban studies and area strategies combine smaller, incremental changes with programmes that aim to enrich and engage local communities. Projects have socially engaged design processes at their heart, bringing life to neglected, run-down high streets and squares in need of rejuvenation.

THIS IS TEMPORARY

In many ways, it is as much about doing and making as thinking: by developing a deep understanding of an urban area, architects can question how we use public space and analyse the needs and desires of the people who live and work there. As the practices here show, this can range from healthy food initiatives and business-ready training for market stall holders to the setting up of an online town team to help crowd-source ideas, or a series of debates broadcast using a radio station. These are not quick solutions to deep-rooted problems, and their effect may not be as quantifiable as more concrete, 'bricks and mortar' projects, but they can help galvanise change and inspire local communities to question, spark debate and propose alternatives.

It could be considered risk-averse, but this type of participatory practice and collective engagement fosters open-ended discussions – a cathartic process to get to the root of the problem, sometimes before considering longer-term, more dramatic changes. The architect effectively becomes the intermediary or translator between the community and municipal institutions, helping to empower residents to take an active part in shaping their communities and opening their eyes to possibilities. It forces the architect to step away from the shackles of a computer screen and get out into the physical world that they are helping to shape – to meet people, have conversations, and 'talk like a human being and not like an architect', as We Made That's Holly Lewis suggests. Yet in these cases, practitioners often no longer have a clearly defined role, but fluctuate between disciplines, as The Decorators – a team composed of an architect, an interior designer, a psychologist and a landscape architect – exemplify. As co-founder Mariana Pestana point outs, the practice's name is significant: 'The Figure of the architect is still a very distant one to the general public, whereas the decorator is somehow more accessible.' Not only is The Decorators challenging existing models of architecture, with new scenarios and situations, it is also proposing an alternative to the traditional architecture practice model.

Particularly in London, public realm projects, such as these over the following pages, came to a head with the Olympic Games in 2012 and centred around the capital's peripheral high streets, with their concentrations of empty shops and deserted civic spaces. High Street 2012 was a complex and ambitious programme to improve and celebrate London's ribbon of high streets from the City to the Olympic Park. It centred on eight area-based initiatives running from Aldgate, through Whitechapel and Mile End, to Bow and finally Stratford, with projects ranging from smartening up shop fronts and redesigning public spaces to hosting mini-festivals and creating new pockets of greenery.

As of 2015, the mayor is in the middle of investing £185 million into London's high streets to boost trade and economic activity, including £120 million from the Mayor's Regeneration Fund, Outer London Fund and Portas Pilot Initiative, £56b million of match funding from public and private sector partners and the £9 million High Street Fund. Not only is this showcased with long-lasting works, the monies support temporary and meanwhile projects in empty shops, disused buildings, vacant land and unloved spaces. The Meanwhile London competition, for example, was launched by the London Borough of Newham and the London Development Agency (LDA) in November 2010 to regenerate empty properties with temporary uses, spawning such projects as Ash Sakula's Caravanserai, an inspiring, five-year, low-budget project and community garden located on a demolition site opposite the transport interchange in Canning Town.

Also leading the way are two resourceful, young and energetic studios, The Decorators and We Made That, interviewed here, both interested in fostering thriving urban environments and public spaces. Following on from its temporary restaurant at Ridley Road Market in Hackney, The Decorators developed an assorted and highly original line-up of strategies and lively events for Poplar's Chrisp Street Market. A purpose-built market square created for the Festival of Britain in 1951, the area was awarded funding from the Mayor of London's Portas Pilot Initiative in 2012 to give the market a much-needed boost and develop local partnerships. Described as a 'research project' by The Decorators, the various initiatives aimed to emphasise the relevance of the market as a public and civic space at the heart of community life. Says The Decorators co-founder, Mariana Pestana: 'We understood that the market had an important economic presence in the area, but that it had also – and perhaps foremost – a cultural relevance. We wanted to emphasise that cultural aspect and ask, "What if the market wasn't only a place to shop but also a civic space?"' In addition to providing new market furniture and communal dining events, The Decorators deployed an empty market unit as a meeting place and community hub, set up a radio station (Chrisp Street on Air) to explore the area's history and hidden stories, organised a series of debates about the future of the market and hosted a programme of activities that ranged from karaoke and film screenings to boxing matches and cookery shows.

Led by the council's public health department, the project was a pilot for future strategies and healthy living drivers at two other attention-starved Tower Hamlets markets, Watney Market and Roman Road Market. The Decorators' recommendations are now being taken up by Poplar Housing and Regeneration Community Association (HARCA) to inform its application for a new round of funding from the Greater London Authority. It is also part of the Specialist Assistance Team for the Mayor's High Street Fund (as is We Made That), a team of 47 consultants across 16 areas of

FIGURE 2.1: previous / Ridley Road Market by The Decorators: A line-up of local chefs created daily menus using market produce; meals were prepared in a ground floor kitchen and raised by a mechanical table up to the guests above
FIGURE 2.2: above / brochures to advertise the events taking place on Chrisp Street market, another project by the Decorators

expertise in six boroughs, that will help with the realisation of regeneration and cultural projects throughout London.

In an area undergoing dramatic change – 750 new homes are planned on Chrisp Street as part of the £2.1bn regeneration of Poplar – the value of The Decorators' project was not only in bringing more people into a cohesive, shared public space, but in supporting local businesses and building relationships between a range of council representatives, developers, residents and shops owners. A town team met regularly, providing an open space to exchange ideas and encourage wide-ranging conversations. In this case, the temporary was a tool to inform and empower the community. The Decorators does not see these projects as an end point, but as a way to create partnerships and build relationships slowly. As Pestana explains over the following pages, they're not quick-fix solutions: 'The value we see in the temporary lies in its relationship with the long-term. What is interesting is that the temporary allows us to test solutions or to interrogate the possibilities of a particular place. Unlike the dominant top-down place-making systems, where somebody decides what the perfect programme should be, the temporary lets the community try it out and listens to their opinion.' Adds Suzanne O'Connell: 'It brings those conversations that are perhaps happening in the council offices, behind closed doors, into a public shared space. It lets you speak to people in their own language.'

We Made That's Streatham Street Manual, likewise, was created to help facilitate ambitious longer-term changes centred around high street renewal and neighbourhood vibrancy. The easy-to-digest manual sets out a range of tangible projects that address the social, spatial and economic possibilities for Streatham High Road as well as providing suggestions for how to raise funds to realise these projects cohesively and incrementally. This includes improving shop fronts, new signage, trial markets, civic stops and high street 'greening', each with a Top Trumps-style estimated timescale and cost. 'The set-up of the manual allows them [the local Business Improvement District in Streatham] to do this in the knowledge that their work will build towards a bigger vision for the area, rather than being piecemeal or uncoordinated,' explains We Made That co-founder Holly Lewis. Elsewhere, We Made That describes its work on the Croydon Meanwhile Use Toolkit as 'facilitatory, rather than temporary'. The project, one of a host of interventions brought about in response to the riots in 2011, encourages and

FIGURE 2.3: left / a radio show taking place with the local community in Chrisp Street Market

enables local people to improve the area by activating Croydon's underutilised, empty spaces with enterprising new uses, that are both low-cost and low-risk – again, empowering the community.

Designed to allow these spaces to be socially beneficial before they can be brought back into commercial use, the project is being delivered as part of the Connected Croydon programme, a series of coordinated public works to improve Croydon's streets, squares and open spaces, funded by the Mayor's Regeneration Fund. An online resource guides people though the process of setting up their own temporary uses with practical steps, resources and case studies. Examples include an outdoor sculpture exhibition, raised vegetable beds on the roof of a car park, and the temporary use of a shopping centre unit as a local museum. Alongside the Toolkit, We Made That also helped Croydon Council to run a Meanwhile Use competition with a £7,000 prize fund as an incentive, as well as a series of supporting workshops covering property, marketing, finance and technology for start-up businesses and community groups. It is further collaborating with landscape practice HASSELL to transform the streetscape of a key gateway into central Croydon – and the heart of the borough's restaurant district – along South End High Street, with enhanced public realm and building frontages. As with The Decorators' Chrisp Street on Air, the project is concerned with how different activities, particularly social and civic functions, can shape our high streets into flourishing spaces and attract both commerce and activity. 'I think the interesting thing here was the interplay between "soft" proposals like the Toolkit, and "hard" interventions like our public realm and building frontage improvements in Croydon's Restaurant Quarter,' concludes Lewis. 'The combination seems to add up to more than the sum of its parts.'

We Made That, though, is particularly wary of the temporary architecture label, and of 'just producing more stuff or making throwaway projects'. Its work aims to give more value to an area and work towards longer-term goals, as it explains in the following interview. Says Lewis:

"We really think that the work that we do can contribute to a better urban environment. Sometimes there's definitely a role for temporary interventions in achieving that – they can build excitement, be used to test ideas and galvanise people. But things that appear and then disappear is not something we've ever been really keen to engage with because we think that the work that we do is worth more than that. [...] There's some commonality between our work and the practice of temporary architecture: there's a concern with the social context of a project, which becomes slightly more potent in a temporary intervention, that we try and capture with other tactics or events."

Public realm projects and community engagement allow more immediate, human-scale action in areas undergoing deep-rooted, permanent change. It helps communities to come to terms with processes that are out of their control. In many cases, creative, tailor-made solutions can help shift perceptions and transform public spaces into much-loved local assets. And as shown in the interviews that follow, rather than developing into permanent solutions, these temporary – or rather participatory – projects test ideas and, ultimately, animate and activate places.

INTERVIEW 03 /
WE MADE THAT

OLIVER GOODHALL /
HOLLY LEWIS

Established in 2006 by Oliver Goodhall and Holly Lewis, We Made That is an
energetic London-based architecture studio delivering all its projects in the public
realm. It aims to make imaginative and considered contributions to the built
environment through socially engaged design processes. The relationship between
local communities, development and creative practice is a particular focus of We
Made That's work and it believes that – handled correctly – interaction can lead
to enriched, exciting and engaging environments. Lewis was shortlisted for the AJ
Emerging Woman Architect of the Year Award in 2012 and is a member of the
Tower Hamlets Conservation and Design Advisory Panel, as well as visiting critic
on the GLA Mayor's Design Advisory Group, while Goodhall is a member of the
South East Regional Design Panel and Hackney Design Review Panel.

How did you meet and start We Made That?

Holly Lewis: Oliver and I met at the Bartlett School of Architecture, UCL, studying for our degrees. In 2006, during our Part 1 work experience, we entered an open competition to design a beach hut for the Lincolnshire coast – and were totally surprised to be one of the winners! It was called the Bathing Beauties competition, and I guess it was basically an arts competition. For the project, you had to submit a model of the beach hut that you were proposing. In the end what they got was hundreds and hundreds of these beach hut models that I believe are still part of a touring exhibition.

We were Part 1 year out students at that point so the incentive to do the competition was not that we wanted to set up an office, it was just because we thought it would be a nice thing to do and that it would be fun. Our design was called A Hut for Gazing and Canoodling. The budget was something like £20,000 to build the thing so suddenly we'd gone from just having a bit of fun, I suppose, to actually 'We have to build this thing!' We Made That started from there and has since grown to become a team of seven working on a whole range of urban projects.

What lessons did you learn from setting up a young architecture practice so soon after you graduated?

HL: It's been an incremental process to grow the practice into what it is today. I think there's a perception that it has to be a great leap from employment to self-employment, but that hasn't been our experience.

What is your opinion of temporary architecture? Where do you see your practice positioned within that world?

HL: We're not interested in producing just more stuff, or making throwaway projects. We really think that the work that we do can contribute to a better urban environment. Sometimes there's definitely a role for temporary interventions in achieving that – they can build excitement, be used to test ideas and galvanise people. But there's a danger that architecture, and the work of young practices in particular, becomes trivialised and undervalued. There seems to be a culture of young architects making expos for oligarchs or jamborees for big brands that we just don't get along with.

We try to avoid temporary architecture in some ways but there have been times when it's been useful. For our recent work in South End, Croydon, the council asked us to produce a few A1 boards that we could put in the window of a shop as part of public consultation about our public realm and building frontage improvements. We said, 'Actually, why don't we take over that unit for a month? We can run events there, invite people in and talk to them.' In a way that was a temporary occupation of a space, but it was related to a wider project, so in that sense it had a value. But things that appear and then disappear is not something we've ever been really keen to engage with because we think that the work that we do is worth more than that. We did a project for a regeneration programme in Blackhorse Lane, Walthamstow, in east London – if you describe all the little parts of the project it may sound complicated or maybe a bit weird, but it involved events and training, billboard campaigns, public realm improvements and shop-front improvements. It's not really all bricks and mortar; I wouldn't

FIGURE 2.4: previous / We Made That's project for Blackhorse Lane included transformations to streetscapes, shops and industrial
        frontages in the area as well as managing a public art commission, 2014
FIGURE 2.5: above / A Hut for Gazing and Canoodling in Lincolnshire, We Made That's first project in 2009

necessarily say that it's temporary but it's 'soft'. We sometimes say that there are 'soft' or social proposals and the architecture is a 'hard' proposal. I think there's some commonality there between our work and the practice of temporary architecture: there's a concern with the social context of the project, which becomes slightly more potent in a temporary intervention, that we try and capture with other tactics or events. There's a strand that ties us in with that world even if we don't necessarily build lots of temporary structures.

Your work deals with the public realm and socially engaged design processes. Could you explain how your design process works and some of the key ideas driving your projects?

HL: All the projects that we undertake are public in one way or another. There's a committed civic ethos behind each one that often involves going above and beyond the typical role of architects to engage people. As the nature of our work expands from design to urban strategies and studies, these tactics also evolve, but we're always keen to make sure that our work is relevant and accessible to as wide an audience as possible.

How did the project for the Streatham Street Manual (2014) come about and what were the ideas behind that?

HL: This was a project for the local Business Improvement District in Streatham, to facilitate them to seek funding and to deliver public space improvement projects incrementally. It is a publication which sets out a range of tangible

potential projects that address the social, spatial and economic possibilities of Streatham High Road in London. The set-up of the manual allows the BID to do this in the knowledge that their work will build towards a bigger vision for the area, rather than being piecemeal or uncoordinated.

Similarly, in 2014 you produced the Croydon Meanwhile Use Toolkit. How did that come about, and what was the thinking behind that?

HL: This was a project for Croydon Council, and was one of a host of interventions that were undertaken after the riots there. The key idea was to encourage local people to feel empowered to improve their area by addressing problems like vacancy on the high street. Our work was facilitatory, rather than temporary, and it involved

FIGURE 2.6: above / We Made That's project for Blackhorse Lane included transformations to streetscapes, shops and industrial frontages in the area, as well as managing a public art commission, 2014
FIGURE 2.7: opposite / locations on Blackhorse Lane singled out for transformations to industrial frontages

producing an online resource to guide people through the process of setting up their own temporary uses. I think the interesting thing here was the interplay between 'soft' proposals like the Toolkit, and 'hard' interventions like our public realm and building frontage improvements in Croydon's Restaurant Quarter. The combination seems to add up to more than the sum of its parts.

What impact do you hope these kind of projects can have on an area in the long term?

HL: We hope that they really do have a positive influence. The Streatham Street Manual is in a way still to be tested – the idea is that there are projects that can be taken off the shelf and fundraised for and that can be taken forward. The UK is just starting to get used to the idea that councils can't deliver everything, so in that case

it's a Business Improvement District and they've got pre-prepared projects that they can go away and hopefully deliver. But because it's an incremental process, delivering a little bit by little bit, you have to wait and see.

The Croydon Meanwhile Use Toolkit is quite an interesting one because it was the council trying to kick off a process whereby citizens would go off and do things by themselves, and actually we ran a competition as part of that with some prize money as an incentive. There's a website which tracks the Meanwhile projects that people have been submitting, because obviously if people are doing things on their own you don't necessarily stay in touch with that. But there have been initiatives such as a new arts charity taking on an empty unit. There are various things going on that we haven't been involved with, that the council haven't put any resources into, but they're

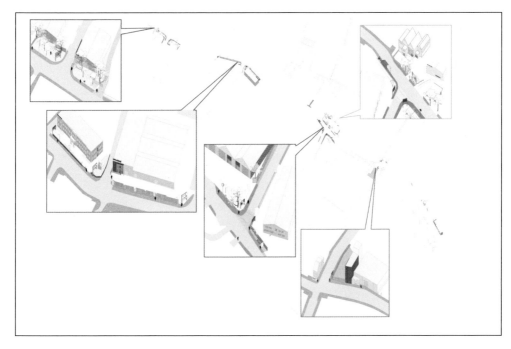

happening anyway and hopefully things like the resources provided by the Meanwhile Use Toolkit helps that to happen. People don't know about things like advertising consent, for example; they're not particularly complicated, but you do have to have somebody to tell you.

How do you engage with the local communities when you do these projects? How receptive are residents?

HL: We always say that it doesn't really matter who you're talking to or where you are, you can always have a good conversation with people about the places they're living in. We did a project a while ago called The Unlimited Edition, producing a series of newspapers in Whitechapel as part of High Street 2012. If you gave out a free paper and said, 'This is a newspaper about urbanism,' nobody would want to take that from

you, but if you say, 'This is about change in the local area,' then loads of people take it. They were genuinely interested and wanted to have that conversation, so it doesn't take much to talk to people. We also always say that you have to talk like a human being and not like an architect, which I think is worth keeping in mind. Architects can talk weirdly sometimes.

Do you think that part of the role of the architect with these urban studies and area strategies is almost to be an intermediary between the planners and the council and the local community?

HL: I think in the sector that we work in, that is sort of how we see ourselves – although we do also think that our design input has value. We don't completely sign over to other people, we bring value rather than just acting as a conduit between

FIGURE 2.8 and 2.9: opposite / the Streatham Street Manual provided practical suggestions for how to raise funds to realise projects cohesively and incrementally, and set out a range of tangible projects

FIGURE 2.10: above / Croydon Meanwhile Use Toolkit encourages and enables local people to improve the area by activating Croydon's empty spaces for enterprising new uses, 2014

those things. But certainly stronger links between those two sides is something that we always try to foster.

Let's talk about the Open Office, the project space you created in The Architecture Foundation in 2013. What were the ideas behind that, and what was the reaction like to the project?

HL: This was a five-week residency exploring the implications of neighbourhood planning for architects. Again, it was really about provoking responses and providing a base for research and events. The reaction was surprisingly positive considering it was five weeks of talking about planning! We had quite a wide range of people engaging with the project, so we had a bunch of architects, planners, representatives from the local authority, but also just regular people.

Some of them brought in files with all these documents of planning issues in their area; some people were really keen to understand a bit more about whether they had a neighbourhood planning group in their area. There was a really wide range of people, and all the events were fully booked, so that was quite a surprise, because I guess architects conventionally aren't supposed to be that keen on planning, but it proved to be really popular.

What issues did it raise?

HL: The idea was to explore the various facets of neighbourhood planning and how it's relevant to architects in particular, so the topics were all based around that. We also had one question a week that we were investigating, and teams of volunteers that came in every week to help us to do that. They ranged from things like 'What does straight-talking planning policy look like?' to 'What does Localism mean for London?'

Looking into the future, where do you see your work progressing?

HL: Recently our work has been expanding to include outcomes such as urban studies, master plans and area strategies – they're not 'bricks and mortar' projects, but they're not temporary either. We want to keep this mix of built work and strategic influence. The end game is the same though: to be respected contributors to the built environment.

What advice would you give to a young student or architect wishing to take a similar route into architecture?

HL: Just do it and see how it goes! I think particularly if you're a student, it slightly depends on what course you're on, but a lot of schools would support you in doing your own thing. I think that there's sometimes an attitude in schools that going into practice is a scary thing to do, or that you won't earn any money – or that you'll just end up doing building regs applications all the time – and I just don't think it's true. I think just grab the bull by the horns!

FIGURE 2.11: top left / the Open Office was a live experimental practice for urbanism hosted in The Architecture Foundation's project space for five weeks in February and March 2013

FIGURE 2.12: top right / the Open Office exhibition created a forum to explore super-local topics relating to the 2011 Localism Act and the emergence of neighbourhood planning

FIGURE 2.13: bottom / Croydon South End Ideas Shop, part of a public realm project in South Croydon to improve streetscapes and building frontages, under construction in 2015

INTERVIEW 04 /
THE DECORATORS

XAVI LLARCH FONT /
MARIANA PESTANA /
CAROLINA CAICEDO /
SUZANNE O'CONNELL

The Decorators is a London-based interdisciplinary group of practitioners set up by landscape architect Suzanne O'Connell, interior designer Xavi Llarch Font, architect Mariana Pestana and psychologist Carolina Caicedo in 2010. It likes to design experiences that invite people to engage with objects and architecture, from a temporary restaurant on Ridley Road Market in Hackney, to a mobile Italian garden at Alexandra Palace and a programme of events, live radio broadcasting and cinema screenings at Chrisp Street Market in Poplar.

How did you start The Decorators?

Suzanne O'Connell: We're all from different backgrounds, we all studied Narrative Environments together at Central Saint Martins, which is kind of about broadening the expanse of how public space should be designed to bring together a range of practitioners. The course had a very strong emphasis on collaboration, and so we all, over the two years, started to like the way each other worked. We then developed a project at the end of second year, once we had finished the course – that was the beginning of The Decorators and we got a studio. We began with a very loose arrangement; before any commissions came along, we worked together on small self-initiated and self-directed projects where we explored and developed an approach to our work. We formed into a company only two years ago.

Where did the name The Decorators come from?

Xavi Llarch Font: I think it's because the first project we did was at 100% Design, which is primarily an interior design fair. The project was an interactive installation and it was a bit tongue-in-cheek. I think the name came up as a reaction to that; it was project-based but we carried on with the name.

Mariana Pestana: I think what is interesting about the name is that decoration is usually seen as a minor form of spatial design, just like the temporary is seen as a second architecture. Another aspect is that the Figure of the architect is still a very distant one to the general public, whereas the decorator is somehow more accessible. Then there is also this interesting thing about the decorator having a double meaning:

the decorator whose job is to design the appearance of rooms and the decorator whose job is to paint or build.

SO'C: We like being embedded in our projects and having an on-site presence.

Let's talk about Ridley's, the temporary restaurant you created in 2011 on Ridley Road Market in Hackney. How did that project come about and what were the ideas behind that?

Carolina Caicedo: Ridley's was a restaurant we built on this 5m x 5m concrete, derelict site, which sat right on the thrall of Ridley Road Market; the site literally overlooked the market traders. The project came about through Atelier ChanChan, with whom we collaborated on the project – they owned the site and had plans for it but wanted to do something temporary while they got planning permission, so we were invited to come up with something. I guess that was the first opportunity for us to really put into practice our approach in some way, or explore the nature of the projects that we wanted to do.

The project developed through just spending quite a lot of time on the market, walking up and down and talking to the traders. It was also quite a visceral response to the site because it was so in contact with the stalls. We instantly felt that we really needed to respond to that or interact with those market traders; we couldn't do something that ignored them or didn't take them into account. There's lots of produce on the market, but primarily fruit and veg, and since that was our raw material, a restaurant felt instantly right.

FIGURE 2.14 and 2.15: previous and above / Ridley's was a temporary restaurant created on Ridley Road Market in collaboration with Atelier ChanChan in 2011

FIGURE 2.16: above top / diners sat at a communal table high above the market
FIGURE 2.17: above bottom / Ridley's was a self-sufficient restaurant, co-existing with the market, the traders and its neighbours

But we didn't want to just build any kind of restaurant on Kingsland Road, as there are now. We saw that demarcation between Ridley Road Market and Dalston: the endless opening up of these hip cafés that weren't necessarily involved with the market traders, for example. We were thinking about how we could make it so that the people who came to the restaurant were also coming to the market and exploring it – to have to engage with it.

We also wanted to involve the market traders in the economy or the system of the operation and the way it worked. So we developed a food-for-food exchange system, where in order to get a cooked meal at lunch you had to buy £3-worth of produce from the market for our ingredients list for the evening meal. Those who came in the evening for dinner when the market was closed got a £5 market voucher to encourage them to return the next day.

Anecdotally, the response to Ridley's was very positive. We sold out our lunch and dinners every day that we were open. We got great feedback from residents and the market traders wanted us to stay longer. We had visits from the local primary school and two site visits from architecture students. We were aware, however, that really only a certain demographic came to eat at the restaurant and if we were to do it again we would work much harder to gather a more diverse range of chefs. At the time we had to work with those who responded. Nonetheless, Ridley's was a very open and transparent space, which meant we were constantly talking to everyone who passed by. By the end of our time there everyone knew us and we felt part of the market.

FIGURE 2.18: right / diagram of the mechanical table that brought food up from the kitchen to the diners on the level above

Another of your projects also involved a London market. Can you tell me about your work at Chrisp Street Market in 2013?

CC: The GLA had been working with Tower Hamlets to think about the revival of Chrisp Street Market and I think they used Ridley's as a case study for the kind of thing that could be done to bring the market back to life.

SO'C: What was interesting about Chrisp Street was that the brief and the management of the project from within Tower Hamlets came from Public Health – they were the ones who had actually pushed for the funding. The idea was how the shared public spaces could actually inform behaviour of healthy eating, so it wasn't just through regeneration, from which a lot of our briefs come. They invited us to present Ridley's and eventually, about eight months later, they invited us to tender.

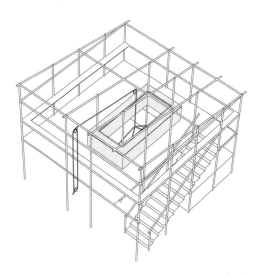

What was your proposal for Chrisp Street?

MP: Chrisp Street was a research project. It was research based on a series of actions that we undertook in the market square. The question we wanted to ask was whether the public space where the market sits could be more than just a place to buy and sell products. We understood that the market had an important economic presence in the area, but that it had also – and perhaps foremost – a cultural relevance. We wanted to emphasise that cultural aspect and ask, 'What if the market wasn't only a place to shop but also a civic space?'

We created a radio show and ran a series of debates about the future of the market. We organised a series of events in collaboration with local cultural institutions, from small ones like the Lansbury Amateur Boxing Club to larger ones such as Spotlight and Bow Arts. In these events we tested different kinds of programmes for the market and in the end we wrote a report and a series of recommendations for the future of the market. Those recommendations are the final outcome of the project. We like to think of Chrisp Street as a research process: it wasn't a solution, it was much more of an enquiry. The recommendations are now being taken by Poplar HARCA, for example, and informing their application for a new round of funding by the GLA, the High Street fund. That is where the recommendations might manifest themselves in something closer to a solution.

FIGURE 2.19: above / The Decorators developed an assorted line-up of strategies and lively events, as well as providing new market furniture for Poplar's Chrisp Street Market in 2013

CC: Alongside that programme we also designed a market infrastructure – new market furniture to host an extension to the different types of activities that we were looking for the market to hold, as a way of also attracting a new audience and bringing in more people.

SO'C: In terms of that infrastructure, I think why we didn't repeat Ridley's at Chrisp Street – which was the original idea – was because there were already successful restaurants there, so we didn't want to come in with another restaurant. It was more about trying to bring people into that shared public space by providing seating and tables that could be used by the restaurants collectively. We then made the Chrisp Street menu, which incorporated all the different menus from the restaurants in the area. It was about using these elements to inform a different behaviour of the

market. The menus, even though a small aspect, were considered a strong output of the project and that's something that Public Health wants brought forward.

What impact do you think these projects can have on an area in the long term?

CC: We don't see the project as the end point. In terms of Chrisp Street, the events and project we did there helped to create partnerships. You can then be more ambitious in the next steps of the kind of things you could do. For example, if we didn't quite feel comfortable building a restaurant to begin with, maybe it's about making a network of restaurants and finding local chefs to open up local kitchens. For us, that was the value of the project.

FIGURE 2.20: above / The Decorators set up a radio station to explore Chrisp Street market's history and hidden stories

MP: During the process of delivering the project a Town Team was formed. This team met regularly and was composed of representatives of Poplar HARCA, the developers Capital Properties, who manage the retail units around Chrisp Street, Tower Hamlets Council, and representatives from Public Health and Enterprise, but then also residents and shop owners, and ourselves. It was really interesting to see the kind of conversations you could have within that context: they were so rich because you could exchange ideas and make decisions a lot quicker. Another important person who sat at the Town Team was the Market Officer, who manages the activities that happen at the market, who is usually someone quite difficult to get to – but here the Market Officer was there right in front of you, so you could negotiate that possibility a lot quicker. The Town Team became this space of potential partnership and collaboration. That was a huge outcome of the project – to create that structure of dialogue. And in the end the biggest question was, 'How can we keep this going?'

SO'C: But, going back to the idea of temporary architecture, allowing this Town Team a relatively small budget to manage – around £100k for the whole project – gives them a strong focus and it builds relationships slowly. Moving forward, that area is undergoing dramatic change but because they've built these partnerships, they're going to have a much stronger role in saying what is going to happen in the future. This Town Team structure has now been used as a case study for other localities because it worked so strongly. A lot of the time there are these stakeholder groups, but they don't have money to manage, they don't have a project. Here, having a project and a clear goal brought a cohesiveness to the area.

MP: The value we see in the temporary lies in its relationship with the long term. However, because the temporary does not need to influence the future directly, in that sense it doesn't have to develop into a permanent solution. What is interesting is that the temporary allows us to test solutions or to interrogate the possibilities of a particular place, it allows us to explore and test – yet such tests aren't just about materiality, form or the construction techniques. We are much more interested in testing programmes and testing the use of particular places.

It's very rewarding to do temporary projects because they allow for a real embodied test from the perspective of the users. Future users can experience the proposal for real. Unlike the dominant top-down place-making systems, where somebody decides what the perfect programme should be, the temporary lets the community try it out and listens to their opinion. It's also very empowering because the decision that the community makes when faced with a consultation process in support of a planning permission would be much more informed. That is, such a decision is not just based on a hypothetical design far removed from their real experience of the everyday.

SO'C: It brings those conversations that are perhaps happening in the council offices, behind closed doors, into a public shared space. It lets you speak to people in their own language.

FIGURE 2.21: opposite top / Chrisp Street on Air at Chrisp Street Market involved a variety of initiatives to emphasise the relevance of the market as a public and civic space at the heart of community life – one example was a boxing match in the market, 2013

FIGURE 2.22: opposite bottom / together with Guglielmo Rossi, The Decorators developed an identity for the project, based on the handwriting of one of the market stall holders. It was used to advertise the events with stencils on the market walls and columns, event leaflets, and a Chrisp Street Menu of the food available in the area

We always try to create what we call a Trojan horse, or framework, that creates the scenario so people feel comfortable.

What does the future hold for The Decorators? How do you see your practice developing over the coming years?

MP: It's funny, we're going to do our first permanent project over the next two or three years, designing two landmarks for Hayes in Hillingdon. Interestingly, we haven't changed our approach in any way because we're doing a permanent project. We are quite keen to continue exploring the methodologies and processes that we've been using so far and we don't want to lose that even if the projects grow in scale.
SO'C: A project we've just completed the first

phase of is The Hackney Circle in Dalston, which was about exploring how Dalston Square is isolating a lot of the older residents in the area. It was really a non-infrastructural project, it was a strategy, and I think it's those types of projects where potentially our research informs the next phase of development that are interesting – it's not architectural, it's more strategic, but in a way it's the same architectural process.

CC: Hackney Circle is still spatial because you're looking at how relationships map out in public space, but we're just not adding to the public space. We're constructing networks, really.

SO'C: What we say with all of our projects is that the infrastructure is there to support the programme we devise; sometimes the infrastructure is already there and we don't need

FIGURE 2.23: above / the Hackney Circle was developed with Hackney Council for Hackney's over-60s and involved a nine
week programme of events to keep older residents involved in the social and cultural life of a new public square in
Dalston, 2014
FIGURE 2.24: opposite / a radio programme, part of Hackney Circle

to build anything. I think what has been interesting is that our practice has grown quite organically, just from a shared interest in public space and how people use and interact with that space – the outcome as temporary to begin with was ideal because it provided that opportunity for research.

CC: I think the way we want to work a lot more, for example, is the way we worked at Chrisp Street, rather than at Ridley's. There we were so aware that the three-week activity had really very little actual impact. It had a lot of conceptual impact, it inspired a lot of conversations and since then it's been used as a case study for a way of thinking about regeneration and place-making, but we are also aware that we want to do much

more than that. How can you use these projects by remaining in a place and actually slowly building on a place? From the lessons we've learnt at Chrisp Street we now have a suite of ideas, ranging from immediate, small-scale, £30k budget, low-risk projects to much bigger projects that could slowly influence the market, but we're doing it by working with the people that are there. I suppose that is what the temporary allows – that human-scale aspect.

PERSPECTIVE /
PARTY ON: THE POLITICAL VALUE OF TEMPORARY

SHUMI BOSE

Architecture is generally considered as a slow and cumbersome discipline, limited in its ability to respond quickly to crises or changing social climates. Read as a medium of communication, architecture's political statements are typically made in exaggerated terms of permanence – consolidating an imperial presence, for example, in mighty agglomerations of stone and brick. When rapid political responses do manifest in urban space – as with the multivalent #Occupy movements around the world – there tends to be little of architectural quality or significance attached. So in the context of the architects and designers featured in this book, and the field of temporary architecture in which they are blossoming, where is the political value?

THIS IS TEMPORARY

Temporal, collapsible and mobile structures have long been associated with activism and the demonstration of new social orders: think of the unbuilt designs of Archigram, Haus Rucker Co or the French collective Utopie. As platforms for primarily social and political activities, their proposals used 'Instant Cities' and inflatable structures to disrupt the status quo, suggesting new ways of living. It is worth remembering that the members of Archigram dreamt up their radical proposals while holding secure jobs at the then London County Council, designing large public buildings like the Southbank Centre. Today, such opportunities are few and far between, and the rise of temporary projects has undeniably given many young architects a real platform to prove their mettle. Particularly after the financial crisis of 2008, the common sense proposal to make 'meanwhile use' of otherwise dormant sites inspired many imaginative proposals from young architects, and allowed the heady possibility of making something real, even if for a little while.

For all the suggestions of radical spontaneity, today's temporary or pop-up architecture is sooner associated with commercial opportunism – the direct production of capital value for someone, somewhere. Pop-up shops are the most obvious demonstration, but also gastronomic destinations, boutique bars and 'incubator' workplaces. To mine history again, Mies van der Rohe's Barcelona Pavilion, possibly the most famous pop-up of all time, was conceived for a commercial expo, and was one of many hundreds of trade fair stands designed by the great modernist. If the commercial colonisation of urban space seems inevitable, it is worth noting that being temporary is key to producing value. Predicated on the 'experience economy', the very temporality of these spaces adds blink-and-you'll-miss-it exclusivity: you have to be there. Accordingly, the architecture must be memorable and emotive, and essentially photographable, so that the experience can at least be prolonged and multiplied through sharing on social media.

The products of temporary architecture therefore straddles two moments: the kaleidoscopic present and the uncertain future. Pre-empting larger forces of gentrification and urban renewal, temporary architecture can act as a means of creating interest, a transition slide for what is yet to come. A cynical reading could view the telltale signs of shipping containers and upcycled pallets as low-cost smokescreens, disguising morally and financially questionable processes of speculative development: behind the painted hoarding and collaboratively designed bench, the big machinery of gentrification and regeneration continues apace, capitalising on goodwill established at ground level. For developers, having one's brand associated with successful creative endeavours – especially public realm and community interventions – is an invaluable hype generator.

Capital itself is amoral; for architecture, the production of value is no bad thing. Yet with political agency comes the recognition that our work, as architects, enables us to engage with larger forces, and that we are complicit with its engines. In the fêting of very real achievements at a small scale, young architects would be wise not to miss out on the bigger picture by using such opportunities strategically. This could mean developing technical capacities, permanent skillsets and career-boosting networks – at any rate, by insisting on the opportunity to infiltrate the machinery of large-scale change. Though not overtly political, most of the works in this book do not lack in social aspiration. New civic meanings beyond market-driven property and planning frameworks are proposed, often providing a facility or service that wasn't there before: the following pages are filled with community workshops, meeting places, and many other inventive examples, sensitively tuned to the needs of specific localities. This is the great privilege of small-scale temporary interventions, especially when undertaken with the youthful chutzpah to stretch tiny budgets, and by architects for whom the zeal of social intervention still seems real.

In such cases, the architect has political agency in highlighting what is essential to the heathy functioning of social and civic life. As opposed to the exclusive world of boutique retail, the fragility of temporary architecture is a reminder of the lack of investment into the permanence of civic and cultural provisions. The precariousness of public services – especially in cultural and creative sectors – is real, and the displacement of workshops, community spaces and after-school clubs into collapsible tents and temporary pavilions, however well designed, may be a problematic reflection of this difficult truth.

But perhaps we would miss a trick by dismissing the power in ephemerality, in the very frivolity of temporary architecture. The literary theorist Mikhail Bakhtin considered the 'carnivalesque' a means to challenge the overarching systems and binary oppositions of life – between public and private, or sacred and profane. Carnival suggests not just the periodic festivity, but rather a temporary disregard for social hierarchies, the inversion of power structures for the sake of delight – elevating the shared experience of communal celebration as a necessary political force. Of course, such disruption can only ever be temporary – but in demonstrating moments of hedonism, of alternative social encounter and shared experience, the temporary can galvanise collective desires and point towards more enduring change, both in societal and built structures. 'The character of the carnival is universal,' writes Bakhtin. It is 'a societal rebirth and renewal, in which everybody participates' towards the political agency of the pavilion party!

What this might mean, in terms of architectural design and realisation, is amply demonstrated in the many joyful, conscientious, generous and (importantly) beautiful projects featured in this book. If architecture's enduring political statements have historically reinforced the orders of power, then today's temporary interventions are arguably more potent, more acerbic and certainly more democratic – allowing architects and designers to interrupt, even for a fleeting moment, the pace of urban change. Indeed, change is the only permanent condition we live in, so forget forever: long live the temporary.

CHAPTER 03 /
PLAYFUL STORYTELLERS:
DIGGING DEEPER
AND BUILDING NARRATIVES

INTERVIEWS:
ABERRANT ARCHITECTURE [UK] / STUDIO WEAVE [UK]

A number of imaginative, young practices are conceiving temporary structures that are backed up by inquisitive detective work into a particular place and the construction of playful but thought-provoking narratives. From dream poems and decorative temples to travelling theatres and fortune-telling chickens, the projects described here draw inspiration from evocative, historical tales and the quirky oddities that make somewhere unique. Yet they're not to be dismissed as light folly: these projects share deeper social aspirations to connect physical structures with people and place.

'We've never done a project that doesn't start with a conceptual understanding, some sort of contextual or social research,' says Studio Weave's Eddie Blake, interviewed in this chapter alongside Aberrant Architecture, 'We try to understand what is actually going on in a place first and react to that.' Adds Maria Smith: 'There's always digging at the beginning. It's what makes every project new, interesting and different. Otherwise you just keep coming up with the same thing over and over again.'

These projects, being temporary in nature, let their creators' imaginations run wild, with the design process allowing for more freedom to test out ideas that will inspire and engage an audience. In permanent projects, such thoughts and narratives might seem superfluous, but with temporary structures, it is a means of talking about serious issues in a more genuine, accessible, fun way. Says Aberrant Architecture's Kevin Haley over the next pages: 'Interaction is quite social or playful, that's something we've learned doing these temporary projects that people really enjoy.' His partner David Chambers agrees: 'I think there is a craving for human, shared experiences and face-to-face interaction, and I think a lot of temporary architecture can pop up and provide those moments.'

Projects of this nature often dig deep into the history of an area, drawing on obscure observations to develop a conceptual understanding of a place. On the surface this may appear light-hearted and whimsical, but these structures can act as metaphors, analogies and symbols of change, bringing together elements of the past, present and future. Studio Weave reveals in its interview that it likes to approach projects from a slightly 'sideways angle' to find a solution to a problem and engage with the local community. Its Paleys upon Pilers, for instance, is an intricate, latticed timber hut perched on slender stilts that was installed in Aldgate to celebrate the gateway from the City of London to the Olympic Park for the London Festival of Architecture 2012. Acting as a beacon for the changes to take place in the surrounding area across the next decade, the temporary structure stood at the start of High Street 2012, the ribbon of streets singled out for major face-lifts on the way to the games site in Stratford.

While looking into the history of the site, Studio Weave discovered that English poet Geoffrey Chaucer had lived in rooms above this historic thoroughfare in the 14th century. During this time he wrote so-called 'dream poems' that included fantastical images of dream-like temples precariously elevated above vast, strange cityscapes. In one poem, 'The House of Fame', he describes a temple of glass filled with golden, decorative images, and a sumptuous palace on a mountain of ice, with a 60 mile-wide spinning wicker house of gossip in the valley – an analogy for the bustling, medieval city Chaucer's own home stood over.

Studio Weave's Paleys draws on Chaucer's dream poems and is an abstraction of his room above the old gate, 'a ghostly base over which new dreams and imaginings can be overlaid'. The delicate structure, marooned on a busy traffic island, and surrounded by the modern architecture of the city, is supported on pillars that are decorated and gilded with a pattern inspired by Chaucer's manuscripts,

FIGURE 3.1: previous / during their research, Studio Weave discovered Chaucer lived in rooms above Aldgate and wrote poems that included fantastical images of dream-like temples that inspired this delicate structure Paleys upon Pilers
FIGURE 3.2: opposite / a sketch of children looking onto the Lullaby Factory at Great Ormond Street Hospital, also Studio Weave

while a wooden owl, named Geoffrey, perched high up on the roof to ward off pigeons. Here, the theoretical idea behind the project brought to a temporary structure a meaning and substance that could easily have got lost in the wider regeneration of the area. The temporal nature of the project also allowed the studio to think more abstractly and develop an elaborate narrative that might, in a conventional permanent project, have been suppressed by more pragmatic considerations. It provided a highly original and thoughtful focal point and stitched together an identity for one of the city's key arteries. The dream poems 'allowed Chaucer, in quite a restricted society, to say really quite far out stuff', notes Blake. 'Like it had for Chaucer, this [approach] allowed us to talk about the delicateness of Paleys. It's an interesting form to talk about quite serious stuff in – "playful" is a dangerous word – an indirect and elegant way.'

Likewise, the Lullaby Factory mediated a situation whereby the multi-phased redevelopment of London's Great Ormond Street Hospital meant that patients' windows looked onto an uncomfortably close, pipe-ridden brickwork façade. But rather than tidying up the ugly space with mere surface decoration, Studio Weave went deeper and made a more profound gesture that could engage the resident children. As with Paleys upon Pilers, it was about creating something playful and imaginative in the awkward intervening period between dramatic change – accepting and celebrating a place's oddities and quirks, and 'rather than hiding what is difficult, creating something unique and site specific'. Studio Weave transformed the space with a fantastical network of copper listening pipes, creating an

FIGURE 3.3: above / curious trumpets fill the awkward space between the two hospital buildings at Great Ormond Street

intriguing and uplifting environment for the recovering young patients to peer out onto. Composer and sound artist Jessica Curry composed a new lullaby for the project, which could be heard though the pipes or from the wards by tuning into a special radio station.

Although Studio Weave is now chasing bigger, and not necessarily temporary projects, often with local authorities and arts festivals, it says that architects such as themselves risk being pigeonholed as creating nothing but temporary pavilions. 'We'll always be interested in temporary projects. There's always going to be temporary and to some extent that will always be associated with promoting ourselves,' says Blake.

Aberrant Architecture, meanwhile, talks of 'design layers' in its work. Not merely concerned with how something looks, it endeavours to provide a captivating and meaningful story – a playful twist – behind, if not at the centre of, every project. 'We like to do projects that can be appreciated as a nice piece of design on a superficial level, but also that have these layers, which mean you can interact with it and get more from it,' says co-founder David Chambers. Always, projects are approached with a dash of humour, a smattering of history and a layer of storytelling, with the aim of reconnecting people in the street and creating 'shared, intimate experiences'. Its bright red Tiny Travelling Theatre, towed by a VW Campervan, toured sites in Clerkenwell for Clerkenwell Design Week (CDW) in 2012 and invited an audience of up to six people at a time to take part in a series of folk performances.

FIGURE 3.4: above / the Small Coal Man's Tiny Travelling Theatre by Aberrant Architecture, a mobile theatre that could fit an audience of up to six people

The practice delved into the history of Clerkenwell and discovered the story of Thomas Britten, a 17th-century travelling coal salesman, who had a small theatre space atop his transportable coal shed where he hosted concerts and plays. 'We were fascinated by this story of a micro-theatre in Clerkenwell. We pitched to CDW that it would be interesting to bring back a micro-concert experience and reawaken the story of Britten for the 21st century,' says Chambers. 'We took cues from little snippets of the information that we could find about the original venue. There were no original drawings or anything, but there were brief descriptions about how you had to duck to enter, and we knew that it had an organ inside.'

As well as references to history, Aberrant's work is also concerned with forming a critical debate about how the way we live, work and play is changing in the built environment today. Says Chambers in the interview: 'What is quite good about temporary projects is that they allow you to test a series of "what ifs". For example, with the Tiny Travelling Theatre, what if the street or space around Clerkenwell could be used for more than just walking, getting from A to B? Maybe it could become a place that we could occupy and a place where you can have these different experiences.'

With Roaming Market, a mobile structure created as part of the rejuvenation of Lower Marsh Market in London Waterloo (Waterloo Quarter's Portas Pilot project), Aberrant was inspired by the 'totem' structures around which traders used to assemble at London's historic street markets and Lambeth's

FIGURE 3.5: above /the mobile Roaming Market in London's Waterloo unfolds to provide a multifunctional market stall and a stage on the roof for performances

history of fortune tellers, mystics and peep shows. The resulting bright blue structure unfolds to provide a multifunctional market stall, featuring covered seating with built-in chessboard and a stage on the roof for performances. A giant chicken sign at the top of the structure reflects stories of chickens being used to tell people's fortunes. Weaving together the richness of the area's past and the street's current character, Aberrant even based their unique style of drawing on Hugh Alley's idiosyncratic 1598 publication *A Caveatt for the City of London*.

Still in use today, the Roaming Market has since been used by fortune tellers for St George's Day celebrations, acted as the world's smallest restaurant – with a kitchen on the roof and a one-to-one dining experience below ('not something we had dreamt of but something that happened as a result of people interacting with the piece') – as well as a signage tool to draw commuters coming in and out of Waterloo Station to the market. Aberrant has continued to add elements to the project, such as a market kit of tables and chairs, and slowly the Roaming Market has become a permanent piece of Lower Marsh. Says Chambers: 'With the Roaming Market, part of its function was as an interface or a way of showing people in the area that actually the market has more to offer – there are these new activities.' Indeed, Aberrant has difficulty defining it specifically as a temporary project: 'While it is a temporary structure, it's a permanent part of the fabric of Lower Marsh,' says Haley. It also sees these temporary projects as part of a seamless portfolio of permanent projects too – 'a continuous flow of knowledge building up' – as the practice has progressed. Like Studio Weave, the practice does not want to be pigeonholed: 'While it has been an evolution, meaning we're getting a bit permanent each time, it's not a one-way street,' concludes Chambers.

As both practices show, the role of the architect in such projects has expanded to include storyteller, historian, anthropologist and communicator. With a focus on the more playful side of research and participation, these captivating works share an intention to reconnect people with their urban public spaces, whether through historical connections or with face-to-face interaction. 'In some ways we are a creative consultancy, we're not just architects,' says Studio Weave's Blake. 'We like selling ideas, and there will always be a market for temporary in that world.'

INTERVIEW 05 /
ABERRANT ARCHITECTURE

DAVID CHAMBERS /
KEVIN HALEY

Aberrant Architecture is a London-based multidisciplinary studio and think-tank set up by David Chambers and Kevin Haley in 2009. Inspired by the way contemporary lifestyles are evolving, Aberrant has established a reputation for playful, provocative and interactive projects, from a tiny mobile theatre towed by a camper van, through an interactive installation built in collaboration with local community groups, to a structure for the world's smallest restaurant. In 2010, Aberrant was architecture resident at the Victoria and Albert Museum and, in the same year, co-founded The Gopher Hole, a gallery/venue in London, which provided a platform for critical debate on the arts and society. It won D&AD and Design Week awards in 2012 and 2013, and exhibited in the British Pavilion at the 13th Venice Biennale of Architecture.

How much of your work would you say is temporary and was it a conscious decision to do such projects when you started Aberrant Architecture?

David Chambers: At the start, all of our projects were temporary but I don't think that was necessarily a conscious decision – 'Let's do temporary projects.' I think those were the opportunities we were presented with. Our first projects were biennales, involving exhibitions and installations, and then they progressed to things that were a bit more permanent. What I think was useful and interesting about those projects is that because they were temporary, they allowed us to test out ideas, get projects made and build up a portfolio of different things in the first couple of years of our practice. If they had been more

permanent commissions, that process would have taken a lot longer.

Kevin Haley: There's been a natural escalation starting with temporary projects then moving onto projects like the Roaming Market, which exists between the realm of the temporary and the permanent. The Roaming Market for Lower Marsh Market in London's Waterloo is a mobile structure that unfolds into a multifunctional market stall, featuring a covered seating area with built-in chessboard and a stage on the roof for hosting events. While it is a temporary structure, it's a permanent part of the fabric of Lower Marsh.

For example, the Tiny Travelling Theatre, created for Clerkenwell Design Week in London in 2012, was also a temporary project, but it's now a permanent piece that we include in other events

FIGURE 3.6: previous / a giant chicken sign at the top of the Roaming Market reflects historic stories of chickens being used on the market to tell people's fortunes
FIGURE 3.7: above / the Tiny Travelling Theatre toured sites of Clerkenwell for Clerkenwell Design Week in 2012

and we very much hope to use it again. The Tiny Travelling Theatre is a mobile structure towed by a camper van, which allows an audience of up to six people to enjoy a series of micro live performances. What amazes me about that whole thing is that unless we had asked to keep it at the end of the three-day event, it is highly likely that the theatre would have found its way into the bin. What I think is a real shame with temporary architecture is that there's no recycling process.

DC: At the moment it's in the yard of the workshop of the fabricator who we use to build a lot of our projects, under a cover, waiting for its next opportunity. We have talked about setting up a website for it to allow people to use it for different things. The interesting thing about mobile projects is that they can become temporary in

different locations but actually they're potentially a permanent thing, they just occupy different spaces temporarily.

Do you think that temporary projects such as the Roaming Market can also have a long-term effect on a local area?

DC: With the Roaming Market, part of its function was as an interface or a way of showing people in the area that actually the market has more to offer, there are these new activities and a greater variety of stalls, it's not just about food.

KH: The Roaming Market has had a massive effect on the area and that's demonstrated in the fact that after we did the project, it attracted attention and they realised that people coming

FIGURE 3:8: above / the Tiny Theatre explored the intense emotion of a micro live performance

FIGURE 3.9: above / the Roaming Market, a mobile structure on Lower Marsh Market in London's Waterloo, hosted fortune tellers for St George's Day celebrations

into the market had nowhere to sit, so we had a separate commission to design a market kit of tables and chairs. We continued adding elements to the project and it's become more permanent.

DC: The idea of temporary and permanence is strange in a way. We're currently working on a public arts commission, a proposal for a civic stage in the museum green in Swansea – that's a temporary commission, but actually it needs to be there for 20 years, so it's classed as permanent. Historically, the area was a hub for the docks and it was a real hive of trade and activity and things going on in the public realm. At the moment they've done a lot of new public realm work, but it's quite sterile and there's not much activation. The idea is that we're building on the legacy of this area and adding something that will help promote this area for people to use for different activities. The fashion department of the university, for example, is talking about using the stage for fashion shows.

But, how long is temporary? In the public consultation one of the members of the public had a bit of difficulty with this concept. She said, '20 years doesn't sound very permanent.'

KH: Why does it matter whether it's temporary or permanent? Surely it's just about measuring the effect. If something is there for three days and it has a great effect on a community, or if something's there for 30 years, does it matter?

DC: I don't know what the definition of temporary is. There's a shrine in Japan, for example, that's mentioned in the Metabolism book that Rem Koolhaas and Hans Ulrich Obrist did. Apparently it's been there for hundreds of years, but every 30 years it gets knocked down and they build

an exact replica of it. Their idea of heritage is different; we in the West, I guess, are a lot more interested in heritage and materials, but for Japan this project is more about the activity or the ritual. The actual physical thing is temporary but the activity or use is very permanent.

And what about the role of the architect? You often describe yourselves as storytellers. Do you think temporary projects provide a different role for the architect, one which allows for more creativity?

DC: I think people are a bit more willing to have something a bit more challenging or a bit more interesting or fun if it's only going to be there for a short amount of time. If people start to think, 'Oh, this is going to be here for 50 years,' they're going to have a different outlook. I think there's a willingness to allow things to be more playful, so I guess in a temporary brief you have a bit more freedom and opportunity to test different things that arguably you wouldn't be able to do if it was there for a much longer period of time.

How does your design process work? Does it involve research into the site or interaction with the community, for example?

DC: I think the best example of interacting with a community for a temporary project is probably Social Playground for the FACT Gallery in Liverpool in 2011. They wanted a way, through an exhibition or installation, to reveal to the museum-going public the consultations and temporary activities they do with different local groups. We did a series of workshops and engagements with groups ranging from primary school children to environmental groups and pensioners. I think we started off thinking, 'Let's get them to make some models,' but in the end we realised that actually a 75 year-old isn't that interested in making models, so we went to the pub and had a few pints instead! In the end, out of those workshops and conversations, we started to design these structures and each structure related to the work that these groups were doing and our research into the histories of the area.

KH: I don't think our design process is different whether we're doing temporary or permanent projects. We always approach a project with a dash of history, a bit of fun. We do place people first – we always look to engage or do some participation event and connect back to a story or history. For the arts project in Swansea, it is a permanent structure but our design has temporary events. Temporary events change all the time so in a way it's doing both. I think the advantage of temporary for a lot of people is that it's something new that's around for a couple of days, it creates this real hype and attention, then disappears, and then you get excited for the next pop-up.

Are accompanying events important to your projects? Are they something you come up with or something the client asks for?

DC: A lot of briefs ask for some level of community engagement. We suggest ideas that we think would be the most interesting way to get results we can work with. A lot of our projects act as platforms for people to engage and interact with. What we normally do is create a storyboard, and what we've been working on with a couple of recent projects is this idea of scripted space – creating a drawing that illustrates how a space could be used and draws the scenarios as suggestions or demonstrations. Then

it's up to the client to program that. I guess the hope would be that these platforms or structures catalyse activities, but I think certainly when we're designing, we're always thinking it would be great for it to be used in this way or that way. I definitely think there's a link between the actual structure and the activity, interaction or occupation that we're imagining or hoping might happen there.

KH: It also changes as well: you can imagine how people might use something, then you build it and they use it completely differently. For example, we've just finished a project in Canterbury called Despite Efficiency: Labour, which essentially is a gallery space where we've lowered a suspended ceiling to the height where you can just pass underneath it in an office chair. We originally thought people would get the chair, go underneath and then stand up to watch the films inside these spaces – however, what people ended up doing was completely different and it became this different use of space (see Figure 3.13). I think that happens a lot with our projects. The Roaming Market we originally designed as a stage, and the next thing I see is a photograph of it being used as the world's smallest restaurant – not something we had dreamt of but something that happened as a result of people interacting with the piece.

DC: It's really quite satisfying when you see that people have taken the structure and riffed on it and created a use that we hadn't imagined, one that's actually better than what we could ever have imagined.

Why do you think temporary projects are popular at the moment?

KH: I think the pop-up and the temporary sits in the right time in society, in the sense that a lot of people crave an update or the new – the way we consume technology, the next 'Facebook check-in' experience, and so on. So the idea of doing something that's only there for three or four days I think really sits well with people's lifestyles. If something stays there for a long time, it can lose its appeal quite quickly. That's something we've found doing with mobile structures: as soon as you move it to a different context it becomes new again.

DC: Also what is quite good about temporary projects is that they allow you to test a series of 'what ifs'. For example, with the Tiny Travelling Theatre, what if the street or space around Clerkenwell could be used for more than just walking, getting from A to B? Maybe it could become a place that we could occupy and a place where you can have these different experiences. To actually redesign a high street would take a long time, but with a temporary project you have an opportunity to little moments. In our practice we've become very interested in

changing lifestyles, how people are increasingly using the city – to live, work and play. The public realm is becoming very important.

KH: I think something else that has come up a lot as well is the idea of interaction. I think when people think about that word, they immediately imagine something digital, and a lot of our projects don't embrace that side of it yet. Interaction is quite social or playful, that's something we've learned doing these temporary projects that people really enjoy.

DC: Maybe it's a reaction to social networks and things but I think there is a craving for human, shared experiences and face-to-face interaction and I think a lot of temporary architecture can pop up and provide those moments.

KH: A lot of times, the design of the piece becomes the icebreaker for that sort of thing to happen. The Tiny Travelling Theatre, for example,

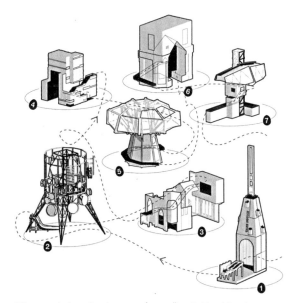

FIGURE 3.10: above / Social Playground is based on the game of egg rolling, inviting visitors to race eggs down seven unique structures

is red and peculiar. People started coming up and asking, 'What is this?'

The other thing that I think is great about doing all these temporary projects isn't necessarily something we set out at the beginning to do, but because a lot of them are at a small scale, it meant we could take on some of the fabrication and build some of them ourselves, which was great as a learning process. When I first started working in practices, out of university, there weren't many opportunities to get physically involved with the fabrication of projects. You'd turn up on site and be expected to understand it. I now absolutely love the making side of things and by taking this hands-on approach I find the process of design from start to finish much more rewarding.

DC: I think it's a common thread in the people you're talking to in this book, this interest in not just the actual design on the computer but the craft of it as well, almost learning by doing. It often allows you to come up with more creative projects.

Do you think you will continue to do temporary projects or were they just a means to win bigger, more permanent projects?

KH: I see our projects as a continuous flow of knowledge building up. It just seems like a continuous thread: you look back and think, 'Oh yes, I guess we have done quite a lot of temporary architecture.'

DC: I don't think we want to be pigeonholed as just doing temporary projects. We've just done a refurbishment within a school, for example, which has been very different from a temporary project. Even though we are moving

on to more permanent projects, though, it's not like we wouldn't want to do temporary things again. I think small, temporary interventions with briefs that allow us to do interesting things can be challenging in a way that we'll always be interested in. While it has been an evolution, meaning we're getting a bit more permanent each time, it's not a one-way street.

FIGURE 3.11: above / the roof of the Tiny Travelling Theatre was topped with coal scuttles

FIGURE 3.12: above / Despite Efficiency: Labour was an installation in 2014 that invited visitors to propel themselves underneath a suspended ceiling into an artificially lit world

INTERVIEW 06 /
STUDIO WEAVE

EDDIE BLAKE /
ESME FIELDHOUSE /
MARIA SMITH /
JE AHN

Studio Weave is a young London-based architecture practice set up in 2006 by

Je Ahn and Maria Smith. It now has seven members of staff, and has created

a diverse range of imaginative and joyful projects: a romantic wooden cabin

on a lake edge in rural Northumberland; a bench that winds its way along

Littlehampton's promenade; a floating cinema; and a timber palace, perched

on pillars, that celebrates Geoffrey Chaucer in Aldgate. Its work has won a

number of prizes including three RIBA awards and the *Architectural Review*'s

International Emerging Architecture Award, while The Longest Bench received

the Civic Trust Awards' Special Award for Community Impact and Engagement.

How did you start Studio Weave?

Maria Smith: We set up Studio Weave in 2006 when we were doing a temporary project, 140 Boomerangs, for the London Architecture Biennale, which then became the London Festival of Architecture. It was just before the recession and Je Ahn and I had been working on a student project, which involved coming up with ideas for making interventions in public spaces along the festival route.

140 Boomerangs comprised a modular element that could be assembled and reassembled in various permutations to create site-specific, fluid, playful forms from one boomerang shape. It first wrapped around the Peace Fountain in West Smithfield and later it was used as play-furniture on Queen Street in the City of London and at each of the three local schools that took part in workshops.

We fundraised to build the project and got some sponsorship for timber. We also got some money from the City of London, so we actually were able to make it happen and that was kind of our degree project. We set up the practice on the back of that really, initially doing quite a lot of public art and public realm things, continuing to work with the City of London, and then gradually building it up since then. We do quite a lot of work for local authorities and arts festivals.

What attracted you to designing temporary structures? How much of your work would you say is temporary now?

MS: What is our definition of temporary?

Eddie Blake: Everything lasts a certain amount of time. Quite a lot of the things we do that are really temporary, designed for a six-month lifespan for example, have still been around five years later. And that's to do with money, and that's to do with people thinking they're going to hedge their bets and just say it's temporary – they get to like it and it's actually a scary decision to say, 'This is going to last a hundred years.' I think there's something in the climate and the culture at the moment, which means we want to do more temporary stuff. But a lot of our work is temporary in that kind of traditional six-month period.

FIGURE 3.13: previous / Lullaby Factory transformed the ugly view from patients' windows at London's Great Ormond Street Hospital with an imaginative network of copper listening pipes

FIGURE 3.14: above left and opposite / Studio Weave's first project, 140 Boomerangs, wrapped around the Peace Fountain at West Smithfield for the London Architecture Biennale in 2006

FIGURE 3.15: above right / 140 Boomerangs was comprised of modular elements that could be assembled and reassembled into various iterations

MS: The Lullaby Factory, for example, at Great Ormond Street Hospital in Bloomsbury, London, in 2013, transformed an awkward exterior space landlocked by buildings. The multi-phased redevelopment of the site means that the recently completed Morgan Stanley Clinical Building and the 1930s Southwood Building – which won't be demolished for 15 years – currently sit uncomfortably close together.

There's a gap of less than one metre in places, and large windows in the west elevation of the new building look directly onto the pipe-ridden brickwork façade of the Southwood Building. Our aim was to reimagine the façade as the best version of itself, accepting and celebrating its qualities and oddities and – rather than hiding what is difficult – creating something unique and site specific. That's one kind of temporary project,

but there are others, like Paleys upon Pilers, which we put in Aldgate, London in 2012. We originally had planning permission for six months, but that was extended and it ended up being there for two years. It came down in January 2015 because the site it was on is planned to be made into a highway. We got confirmation that the structure will move nearby though. That's nice because the reason is that it is liked, someone wants to take it.

EB: There's a good example at the other end of the spectrum: The Midden, an artist's studio on the West Coast of Scotland, which the client wanted to last over 100 years. That means we have to go to extraordinary lengths when we're doing the structural engineering: it has to survive not just a 100-year storm but a 1,000-year storm. But she also said that if someone does decide to take it

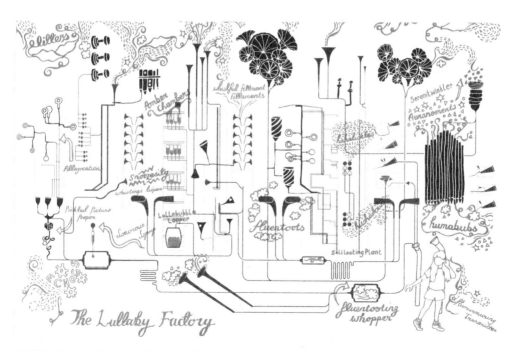

FIGURE 3.16: above / schematic sketch of the Lullaby Factory

away, she wants there to be no scratch on the landscape. We designed it in such a way that it is just plugged in and it's not carving into the land.

MS: Proportion-wise, maybe a third of our projects have been temporary. Not so much now, but in the earlier days, we did quite a lot of temporary projects. It's not Meanwhile frenzy any more.

EB: It seems like we are getting fewer. I think we're chasing bigger projects and when people spend millions of pounds, it's not going to be temporary. But then we do always get approached for projects like Smith at Clerkenwell Design Week in London in 2014. Smith was a pavilion and exhibition that showcased the innovative use of tools in making, from historic crafts to contemporary fabrication techniques.

During CDW, contemporary craftspeople and smiths took residence in Smith, hosting a number of workshops and demonstrations. The pavilion itself was made of fibre-cement panels, a material invented by re-appropriating an old paper mill and spinning-machine.

That's always going to be temporary and to some extent that will always be associated with self-promotion. In some ways we are a creative consultancy, we're not just architects. We like selling ideas and that sort of thing, and there will always be a market for temporary in that world.

MS: We've done some stuff for performances as well and that's inherently temporary.

EB: We did one project that was a funny West End production of contemporary dance. It was in

FIGURE 3.17: *above / composer and sound artist Jessica Curry composed a new lullaby for the Lullaby Factory, which could be heard through the pipes or from the wards by tuning into a special radio station*

FIGURE 3.18: above / the Lullaby Factory incorporates old tap and gauges reclaimed from a hospital boilerhouse that was in the process of being decommissioned

a deconsecrated church on Shaftesbury Avenue, and we basically designed a set you could dance with, the set moved; it was very light, beautiful and made of aluminium. The point was that it could all get packed up. This is the edge of architecture, where it becomes set design, but it's definitely temporary, we definitely used an architectural understanding to make it happen. And although it's moved around – the structure still exists – it is never going to be in the same place.

Let's talk about Paleys upon Pilers in Aldgate in 2012. How did that project come about and what were the ideas behind it?

MS: Originally, for the London Olympics 2012, the marathon route was going to go along the High Street 2012: it was going to go up Aldgate and end up in the stadium. I think when Peter Murray first started thinking about putting something there it was going to be a gateway between the City of London and the Olympic Park. That changed, but it was the beginning of High Street 2012 and Olympics 2012.

He asked us to have a look at putting something on there that commemorated this site in some way. We started looking into the history of the site. Aldgate is actually one of the four original Roman gates, so it's been a gateway for a very long time, but we felt that to build some sort of formal response to Aldgate or to the Roman gate was a bit too direct. So we did some more digging and discovered that Geoffrey Chaucer used to live in the rooms above the gate as a custom's official, which was his day job. We read the

FIGURE 3.19: above/ Smith was a pavilion and exhibition that showcased the innovative use of tools in making, from historic crafts to contemporary fabrication techniques

poetry that he wrote while he was living there, and sleeping there, and eating there, and being absorbed in this kind of tiny little room with a crazy world beneath. That motif just kept coming up in the things that he wrote while he was there: he described these very intricate structures on impossibly slender pillars, above a mad landscape. He called it dream poetry. The format was that you fall asleep and then you have a whole experience and you wake up and think, 'Ah, I'm enlightened.'

EB: Calling it a dream poem allowed Chaucer, in quite a restricted society, to say really quite far-out stuff. You can be satirical and analytical through those dreams. Like it had for Chaucer, this process allowed us to talk about the delicateness of Paleys, and how it's on spindly legs and could break at any time. It's an interesting form

to talk about quite serious stuff in – 'playful' is a dangerous word – an indirect and elegant way.

MS: Are you saying a temporary project is like a dream? I like that.

EB: Kind of. I'm just saying there's a parity between the content of the theoretical idea – 'This is what we are going to do about Chaucer' – and also the production. The project is like the thought.

Is that typical of your design process, that you have these theoretical ideas, a period of research?

EB: Yes, always, with ideas. We've never done a project that doesn't start with a conceptual understanding, some sort of contextual or social

FIGURE 3.20: above / during the festival contemporary craftspeople and smiths took residence at Smith, hosting a number of workshops and demonstrations

research. We try to understand what is actually going on in a place first and react to that.

MS: There's always digging at the beginning. It's what makes every project new, interesting and different. Otherwise you just keep coming up with the same thing over and over again.

How do your projects involve the community? Is engagement important to you?

EB: Yes, incredibly.

MS: I like to point out that we never ask the community or the client to design something for us. At the start of a project we do quite a lot of engagement and creative workshops, and the aim is to understand the nature of the site, the nature of the problem, understand what's going on there really and get under the skin of things. We try to come at that at a slightly sideways angle, so we've done finger knitting, stool-making… Often craftsy, making, hands-on things work really well and it just allows a conversation to happen.

EB: The point is that we are the professionals, we do the design. It's about finding out the problem and that's engagement. It's where a bit of co-design comes in, to really dig down into the client brief.

MS: We're always trying to find new and silly ways to do that. It depends on the environment that they're working in but sometimes you can push it and do quite silly things. We even did an opera once.

EB: If the client's much bigger, a developer or a local authority, community engagement is part of their built-in process that they have to do, so you

can use it as a tool to make it better. It doesn't have to be a questionnaire. You use the fact that it is in the brief to do something more interesting: it's not just consultation, it's engagement.

MS: We've done a lot of work with local authorities, and for public realm projects there's not just one client. You have to try and establish a general, representative idea of what the public around that area needs.

What impact do you think these temporary structures can have in the long term?

EB: Massive. There's a natural conservatism in people's minds – that's a broad statement, I know – but if they can see it and know it, they're more likely to think that it's all right. Trying to introduce people to brand new ideas, such as repedestrianising a whole high street, is dangerous – but to test it, put something there and say it's only going to be there for six months, let people understand it and criticise it, maybe tweak it as well… You're far more likely to get a positive, long-term project if you start with a bit of temporary. It's a cliché, but the Eiffel Tower was temporary. I think once people learn to love a thing, they don't want to let it go.

What happens to a lot of your projects afterwards? Do they have an afterlife?

MS: The first project we did ended up being used as street furniture. Sometimes things do get destroyed; we try to have a legacy as much as possible, but it is difficult. It's very hard to make something that isn't going to cause any waste at all. With the Floating Cinema, for example, which navigated the waterways of the five London Olympic host boroughs during the summer of 2011, we knew it was going to be a temporary

FIGURE 3.21: above / Paleys upon Pilers was inspired by the dream poems Geoffrey Chaucer created while living in rooms
        in Aldgate

project, so rather than building the boat, we leased it, and the people who own the boat now have a better boat.

What advice would you give to other young architects who are hoping to follow a similar route into architecture?

MS: We did a lot of this because we didn't have rich uncles who wanted us to build them extensions.

EB: I think it was also a time, an era.

MS: We could apply for that work. There are online procurement websites and things, it is more accessible.

EB: Also, I guess more negative advice is that it can mean you can get trapped in doing

temporary projects. We still get a bunch of phone calls asking us to make pavilions. It can take a while to progress from public realm and pavilions if you start on that level; people know what you're doing and they ask for the same thing again. If you start with private residential there is the same trap.

MS: You have to be very careful – people often give temporary projects to young architects and think they can pay young architects very little (or not at all!) because they're building up their portfolios.

EB: Often temporary projects cost more in a lot of ways. There are more complicated logistics, often architects are more involved, so often our fees need to be higher.

MS: The fees are disproportionate to the build cost, so it's very difficult to justify. It's not

FIGURE 3.22: above / the latticed structure stood on a traffic island in the centre of Aldgate

FIGURE 3.23: above / Paleys upon Pilers against the nearby Gherkin

necessarily cheaper to make something that isn't going to last. If it's going to last more than a couple of weeks you still need to make it out of steel that isn't going to rust, you can't just slap it up in cardboard. The whole design process and the materials still need to have integrity.

EB: It feels like we're still trying to figure out how to make that work and to be very clear that the client is not making a massive saving by doing something temporary. You've got all these other things to take into consideration; you've still got to pay the engineer the same amount, you still have to make sure the same permissions are in place.

MS: There's very little repetition – it's not like you're figuring out a detail and doing 200 of them. And often everything is exposed, there's no store cupboard where you can hide everything.

So, going into the future, will you continue to do temporary projects or was it a means to win work at the beginning?

EB: We'll always be interested in temporary projects. I also think that maybe we've become quite good at them, because we've worked out a few of the specific problems with making temporary things and so we could probably offer a better service to a client.

FIGURE 3.24: above / an old barge was reimagined as the Floating Cinema in 2011

CHAPTER 04 /
COLLECTIVES AND SELF-INITIATED PROJECTS: MAKING IT UP AS YOU GO ALONG

INTERVIEWS:
Assemble [UK] / EXYZT [France and UK] / Practice Architecture [UK]

A handful of up-and-coming, driven young architects and designers are eschewing traditional modes of education and practice in favour of a more resourceful, hands-on way of building. Paving the way are multidisciplinary collectives such as Assemble, EXYZT and Practice Architecture, all interviewed here, who pride themselves on self-initiated and self-built, temporary projects that engage communities in the making process and rely on collaborative teamwork. For some – EXYZT in particular – it has become a way of living: migrating from one project to the next, inhabiting a space and becoming as much a part of the local community as the structure itself.

THIS IS TEMPORARY

At the heart of each project, though, is a social ambition to propose how urban public spaces might be occupied and used. Certainly, it's about exchanging ideas, thinking on your feet and learning on the job.

Pragmatically, it's about simply getting out there and getting your hands dirty. Founder Nicholas Henninger describes EXYZT, which was originally formed in France, as a collective project rather than a studio or architecture practice. 'We're not working alone as a brand or as a company,' he says, 'the collective is basically a residency that we open to others.' Furthermore, EXYZT's manifesto proclaims it a 'platform for multidisciplinary creation', involving a motley team of artists, graphic designers, photographers and filmmakers, with the aim of challenging the widely held notion of architecture as an independent field of practice. Instead, various participants, often spread across different cities and countries, come together to collectively conceive and organise temporary 'experimental living ventures' that are then inhabited completely. Always, local communities and the public are invited to appropriate the projects, creating a (non-digital) social network and a place for exchange. It says: 'We want to build new worlds where fiction is reality and games are new rules for democracy. If space is made by dynamics of exchange, then everybody can be architects of our world and encourage creativity, reflexion and renew social behaviours. Architecture can expand into a multidisciplinary game where everyone brings his own tools and knowledge to contribute to a collective piece.'
Inspired by Roman baths and Turkish hammams, which historically provided a setting for social

FIGURE 4.1: previous / Amphitheatre in the New Art Centre, Roche Court, Wiltshire in 2010
FIGURE 4.2: above / Southwark Lido by EXYZT transformed a derelict site awaiting development on Union Street into a temporary lido in 2008

gathering and uninhibited political discussions, EXYZT created the temporary Southwark Lido for the London Festival of Architecture in 2008 with filmmaker Sara Muzio. Located on a derelict site awaiting development beside the railway on Union Street, the scaffolding structure provided a water deck, saunas, paddling pools for children, beach huts doubling as changing rooms, living pods for staff and a mobile garden that was then distributed throughout the neighbourhood at the end of the festival. It brought to life EXYZT's strategy of urban renewal, based on the idea that the key to a vibrant city is a community of users actively forming and interacting with their built environment. Each of its projects is seen as a 'playground' for cultural engagement, where stories can be related and told freely. At the time, temporary architecture as we know it in London was relatively in its infancy, prior to developers and councils grasping the narrative potential of vacant sites during periods of construction inactivity, and before the Olympics and High Street 2012 provided an impetus for transitory urban interventions. Founding members of both Assemble and Practice Architecture worked on Southwark Lido as students. Henninger believes the project opened up possibilities for similar sites across the city, in the flux between empty lot and transformation. 'Nowadays people in various organisations still remember this project, because it helped a lot of different organisations or young architects to see what temporary projects can look like. It created confidence – I think that's important. It's not looking at this project as a piece in itself; it helped contribute by breaking the ice a bit.'

It also meant that landlord Solid Space was happy for EXYZT to return to the same site in 2012 for The Reunion. For that, again, a broad range of participants collaborated to create a playful, open-for-all outdoor space, with paddling pools, saunas, handmade tables and chairs, and a stall under one of the railway arches selling locally brewed beer, all inspired by the traditional British public house. Says Henninger: 'It stayed open for two months, so we invited people to propose activities here, but then we left a lot of room for people just to turn up.' Having built up a close relationship with the local community, and created two hugely successful projects, EXYZT will once again hold onto the site until 2016. The project as a whole, in all three iterations, has enabled local people to be part of the conversation around the site's development and has proposed how they might come together as a community. 'I'm looking at this concept of a convenience room for the neighbours,' he says, adding, 'I think that this kind of practice is a real tool to be able to test the ground, test ideas and test the occupation of a space. Temporary projects focus on the human scale, rather than the big infrastructure of a building.'

Similarly, London-based Turner Prize winner Assemble is a design and architecture collective with a belief in the importance of addressing the disconnections between the public and the process by which their urban spaces are made. By involving the public as ongoing participants from the conception to the creation of a project, Assemble champions an interdependent, collaborative style of practice. Founded in 2010 by a group of Cambridge graduates and now comprised of 16 members, Assemble has become a new model for architecture graduates frustrated with the traditional, long-haul route to architecture. Says founding member Amica Dall, 'Assemble has evolved, project by project, to become a collective way of working and a set of shared resources. There is no hierarchy within the organisation, either between people, between projects, or between different skills, outputs and ways of working.'

THIS IS TEMPORARY

Their first project together, The Cineroleum – a cinema housed in a derelict petrol station in Clerkenwell for three weeks in 2010 – came out of the frustration they felt during Part 1 year out practice. 'Working in a more holistic, polymathic role felt more relevant and exciting. We wanted to be out in the city and learning about everything, doing more, in a more immediate way. Above all, we wanted to make something together,' Dall says. 'Self-initiated, self-built projects freed us up to do that.' Built by more than 50 volunteers through a 'process of collective learning and trial and error', The Cineroleum was largely made of cheap, reclaimed or donated materials. Despite being handmade, its details were skilfully resolved, inspired by the decadent interiors that greeted audiences during the golden age of cinema: flip-up seats were made out of scaffolding boards, while a shiny silver, black-out curtain strung from the forecourt roof was fashioned from roofing material. Explains Dall, 'We never thought about The Cineroleum primarily as a temporary project. We just did as much as we could with what we had to hand in terms of time, opportunity, resources and experience. We wanted to find out what was possible.'

Folly for a Flyover was another temporary project, transforming a disused motorway undercroft in Hackney Wick into a new public space that hosted a programme of workshops, film screenings and performances. Again, it was hand-built by a group of volunteers (over 200 on this occasion) using reclaimed or donated materials, this time clay bricks and wood supported by a scaffolding structure. After its nine-week appearance, the materials were reused for new play and planting facilities at a local primary school, while the London Legacy Development Corporation later invested in much-needed permanent infrastructure to allow the space to continue as an events and cultural public space. As with The Cineroleum, hands-on making was of huge importance, not only in the physicality and craftsmanship of the structure, but also in making things happen in the public realm – working with the local community to create something connecting them back to a city's neglected public spaces. 'A lot of the joy of making these projects was in sharing them,' adds Dall.

EYXZT alumni, London-based Practice Architecture also work in a very informal, make-do way – neither of the two founders, Cambridge graduates Lettice Drake and Paloma Gormley, is a qualified architect and they have never had professional insurance, instead preferring to base their projects on

FIGURE 4.3: above left / Frank's Cafe by Practice Architecture has become a popular destination and regular event in the summer calendar since 2009
FIGURE 4.4: above right / all hands on deck to get the red PVC roof of Frank's Cafe up

trust and mutual responsibility. Like EXYZT and Assemble, they are highly driven and resourceful – they make and build all their projects themselves, collectively with friends, family, students and volunteers. 'We see our work as a continual process of learning,' they say, 'We are a group of people making something happen.' This process means that rather than learning from someone else, they're inventing solutions to their own questions, accumulating knowledge in an organic way, and taking on a greater level of accountability and responsibility than their conventional peers. 'There is a lot more space for risk in temporary projects,' they also note in the interview, 'They offer a place to experiment and to be inexperienced.'

Frank's Cafe, a temporary summer bar on the roof of a multi-storey car park in Peckham, was their first project together. Inspired by the possibilities highlighted by their work with EXYZT on the Southwark Lido, Practice used a similarly open, collective way of building. Made for under £5,000, from old scaffolding boards and red PVC held in place with giant ratchet straps, it was built for young Peckham-based arts organisation Bold Tendencies to accompany their summer sculpture exhibition. Following its first outing in 2009, the red tent-like structure has made a regular appearance each summer, becoming the go-to gathering place for ultra-hip twentysomethings. Practice has also since gone on to create displays for exhibitions, bike stands and, on the lower floor, an auditorium built from bales of straw. Say Drake and Gormley, 'There was a fearless energy around at that time and a collective sense that a lot was possible. The car park was this playground, lawless and full of people making, building, trying things out, helping each other... It became a very public and accessible demonstration that young people can have an impact on the city and can make their own place in it.'

All three collectives or groups are broadening the scope of architectural practice and working on their own terms. It may be a bold, risky approach, but even with the chaos and creativity each project brings, each has been a sensitively thought through attempt to make places for shared experiences. And with spiralling university fees, higher education cuts and calls for an architectural education overhaul, this approach could also be seen as a model for engaging architecture students with a more immediate, practical, hands-on experience. It demonstrates that there are other, equally valid ways of doing things – and that it's not just the top 10% of architects who are truly making a mark on our built environment. As Practice Architecture says: 'Perhaps we wouldn't have been able to do so much if we'd started with the intention of setting up an architecture practice, which immediately conjures images of a fixed work place, filing systems, contracts and salaries – things which might have distracted us from, and made us more apprehensive about, just getting on with it. What has defined that experience has been working with our peers, taking risks and continuing to dream a bit, believing that things are possible and you don't have to accept the territory you are given.'

INTERVIEW 07 /
ASSEMBLE

INTERVIEW WITH:
AMICA DALL / JANE HALL

Assemble is a London-based, multidisciplinary collective working across architecture, design, art and research. Founded in 2010 to undertake a single self-built project, Assemble has since delivered a diverse body of work at a range of scales whilst retaining a non-hierarchical and cooperative working method. Made up of 16 founder members under the age of 30, Assemble works from Sugarhouse Studios, a collaborative workshop space which it runs and shares with a company of carpenters and stonemasons, and 12 other individuals and small business. Recent projects include the Baltic Street Adventure Playground in Dalmarnock, east Glasgow, created in collaboration with local children and families, and a sustainable vision for terraced houses in Toxteth, Liverpool, both of which led to being nominated for – and winning – the 2015 Turner Prize.

How did you all meet and start Assemble? What was your primary aim in setting up the studio?

Amica Dall: Most of us met while studying together from 2006 to 2009. We worked together as a loose group for a year and half, without any idea that the group might formalise. The company itself was the product of necessity: in 2011 we received a grant to support a second project together, and had to constitute as a legal entity to accept it. The company also gave us access to the infrastructure we needed to work comfortably as a group at that scale – like insurance and a bank account.

Everyone who was involved in the conversation at that point is a director of the company, and Assemble has evolved from there, project by

project, to become a collective way of working and a set of shared resources. There is no hierarchy within the organisation, either between people, between projects, or between different skills, outputs and ways of working. For all but four of us, Assemble is now a full time occupation, with some people doing Assemble project work alongside teaching or research. It is an infrastructure that allows us to determine not only what work we do, but develop ways of doing it that are rich, enjoyable and allow more extended ways of engaging with projects. It is also a space for developing ideas and interests that don't necessarily have an immediate output. It has no independent mission outside of this, and will survive for as long as it continues to support each of us to do the work we want to do, and enables a collective process which makes us more than the sum of our parts.

FIGURE 4.5: previous / Turner Prize-winning architecture collective Assemble on site at the Yardhouse
FIGURE 4.6: above / the Cineroleum was a temporary cinema in a derelict petrol station for three weeks in Clerkenwell in 2010

What lessons did you learn from setting up a practice shortly after graduating?

AD: The practice evolved very gradually and in response to the needs and demands of the work we were doing, as well as the ideas and skills of those involved. Assemble has grown up like a child.

The first few years were a bit of a fight and a bit of an improvisation. We have developed a structure, which means we can run a practice to support our work, rather than working to support our practice. We are very alive to the challenge this holds, particularly as, five years in, our personal needs become more complex. But it matters – the conditions of production have a very powerful effect on the end result.

Did you set out to create temporary structures or did things just happen that way? And what made you choose to go in the direction of temporary?

AD: We never thought about The Cineroleum primarily as a temporary project. We just did as much as we could with what we had to hand, in terms of time, opportunity, resources and experience. It was relatively unselfconscious; we wanted to enjoy making something and for other people to enjoy it with us. We wanted to find out what was possible.

The idea to try and do a project together came directly out of the limitations and frustrations many of us felt during our first year in practice. At school we had been encouraged and enabled to think about architecture in a very open way, playing at taking part in every part of the project from conception to fabrication. For those of us from different backgrounds, like theatre, philosophy, politics, anthropology and fine art, we had all experienced this in different forms. From that first year in practice, it seemed to us that most practising architects only participate in a small part of the process of creation, and involvement often only starts after most of the more critical decisions have already been made.

But in 2010, when we started working together, developing those skills didn't feel like the most pressing thing, or at least not the only pressing thing. Working in a more holistic, polymathic role felt more relevant and exciting. We wanted to be out in the city and learning about everything, doing more, in a more immediate way. Above all, we wanted to make something together. Self-initiated, self-built projects freed us up to do that, and gave us the chance to be part of the whole life of a project, from working out how to make it possible in the first instance to understanding the consequences of our design decisions, by both having to fabricate them ourselves and then living and working with the outcome whilst running the projects. It underscored some doubts in some areas and gave confidence in others. Naivety is a good teacher.

Conceptually, temporary is a difficult category. I think it has little internal coherence. We all want to live in places that are responsive to our changing needs, and we all need an amount of certainty and permanence to live comfortably together. We would like to live in a world where anyone could take command of the spaces they lived in and among, to make and do things both for joy and out of need, for as long or as little as they wanted. This idea is both intuitive and has a long and deep history. Temporariness, as such, isn't really a problem.

The problem is the uses people put it to: to sell things, to sell themselves, to privilege spectacle over studied response, to abdicate the longer term responsibilities, to avoid difficult questions, to stick a plaster over the chronic difficulty most people have of accessing space in big cities, as a trompe l'oeil for a lack of a particular set of concerns in a longer term plan – these things are the problem. In some discussions, temporary itself has become a cipher for these things, but I don't think it's a helpful one. To some degree the level of attention given over to temporary work as such compounds this. It matters what a project does and how it does it, and it matters that the mode of development and the time frame is appropriate to the ambition.

How many of your projects are self-initiated and how many are commissioned? Has it changed over time?

AD: We are learning constantly, and our projects are growing in scale, ambition and complexity. Since our second project we have been incredibly fortunate in the number of interesting commissions we have been able to access, and for a while these kept us interested, motivated and excited enough to leave less room for speculative development. Overall, the balance has been one-third self-initiated to two-thirds commissioned. Two interesting things have happened: we have started to be commissioned as artists, which gifts a level of freedom that sits somewhere between self-initiated and traditional commissioning. Secondly, we are developing our structure and

FIGURE 4.7: above / the cinema was largely made of cheap, reclaimed or donated materials. Flip-up seats were made from scaffolding boards and the shiny black-out curtain was fashioned from roofing material

way of working together to make more shared time, and this will, I think, lead to more self-initiated work, probably on a larger scale.

What are the benefits of self-initiated projects? Are there many challenges?

AD: There is challenge everywhere. It often comes down to being able to pick our own battles. Working with and for people brings extraordinary opportunity to learn from them, to grow sensitive to new things, to find things you weren't already looking for. In my experience, self-initiated work that is worth doing generally finds its own client pretty quickly – it becomes for something and someone. So I would say the distinction is less pressing than it might seem. The key thing is to work in an environment where you can pursue an idea for its own sake.

How did the project for The Cineroleum in London come about, and what was the idea behind it?

AD: The coincidence that the golden age of cinema was also the golden age of the car felt like fertile ground, as did thinking about the cinema as primarily a social space, and one that was pushed out of the town centres by the car. The tension between the escapism of watching the film and being on a noisy two-lane road on a Friday night (and on a seat that might give you a splinter) was fun. I suppose it has a kind of nostalgic logic to it, but love for film is a great leveller.

Did you build the project yourselves? What was that experience like?

AD: We all like making things, or making things happen. It is what brought us together in the first place. It's not always appropriate to build

everything ourselves, but making can happen on many levels, sometimes simultaneously – from developing a surface treatment or building 1:1 prototypes, through to working as design-and-build contractors. Making can also be making things happen, and therefore be about a process, developing organisational infrastructure and working with people to enable them to make something come real.

Making can be a good way to establish continuity over stages of work, a rich and constantly evolving way of relating to projects. It demands a level of commitment and involvement with the work, which ultimately is its own kind of reward. The economics can be quite complicated, but we are both working on this collectively and making space so each project works this out in its own way.

We are very fortunate to have a big studio with wood, metal, and casting workshops, assembly and testing space and a yard, and using these, even if only to sketch something out to scale, is a really important part of it all.

Seeing as many of your projects are temporary, what happens to your projects afterwards? Do some stay longer than they are first intended or do some get recycled for example?

AD: Some of our projects are temporary – I'd say about 25%, although the proportion is falling. Three of the four large-scale temporary projects were built of clad scaffolding, so re-use of the structure doesn't come into it: you just take it down and it goes back out into the world. Other parts of the project have been used to make new work, and the recuperability is designed into the initial use.

FIGURE 4.8: above / Folly for a Flyover was hand-built by a group of 200 volunteers using clay bricks supported by a scaffolding structure

FIGURE 4.9: above / Folly for a Flyover transformed a disused motorway undercroft in Hackney Wick into a new public space for workshops, film screenings and performances in 2011

The bricks from Folly for a Flyover, for example, are now part of a landscaping scheme at a primary school playground. Lots of material gets re-used through the studio. We also take in materials from other places and projects and put it to new use. Having the space and facilities that we do makes it possible to do this. Although important, the discussion about resources is also slightly off the point. In principle, building things for one-off use sounds like a terrible waste of resources, but no one has to think too long or too hard to think of a dozen permanent buildings that are in whole or part a terrible waste of resources. This is not by any stretch meant to justify temporary projects being wasteful – quite the opposite. We need to apply these standards everywhere.

The other thing to say is that our first few bits of work were only in part structures. Equally valuable to us – and an equally important part of what they were – was what they did, as active, living places made up of long processes starting with collective building, and stretching through making food, building furniture, running a bar, performance, workshops, managing. A lot of the joy of making those projects was in sharing them. If you let go of the exclusive emphasis on structure and think about what was produced as a way of working, a set of relationships, a demonstration of possibility, the temporariness starts to look more background. It also depends on how you frame these projects. As participatory art projects, they have probably quite a long shadow. As buildings, they are rather short-lived. I'm not sure to what extent this is an active thing, but I do think at their best, these kinds of projects can provide a prompt to think about the role of architect and architectural education. That's probably where they are most interesting.

How did the project for Folly for a Flyover in London come about, and what were the ideas behind it?

AD: Folly grew directly out of The Cineroleum. Now that we had some understanding of the momentum it was possible to build up around a project of that nature, we experimented with trying to use our experience as part of a broader public realm strategy. The site was scoped by muf architecture/art as a potential new public space for Hackney Wick, part of the new infrastructure around the Olympics. It was effective on some levels and not on others. The space now has a permanent raised terrazzo surface; it feels safe and open, and it's accessible and available to use in a way that was difficult to imagine before.

What does the future hold for Assemble? Will you continue to design temporary structures or do you see them as a way to get work built quickly and win bigger projects?

AD: Temporary things have a role within projects with longer time frames, too. And probably more importantly, they still have as much power as they ever did to rupture, test and examine how things are – if they are done well. The tool is as good as the person wielding it. Just look at the effect the Red Shed has had on the National Theatre and the South Bank.

We are not currently working on any temporary projects, aside from interim use workspaces. Apart from this, there are a few ideas which we have been working at for a while which are temporary in the sense of not being permanent built work. For example, we've been working away at rather a far-fetched plan to close Bow Interchange Flyover for a street party, like a cross

between critical mass and a village fête. There are a couple of projects which are longer term and include a kind of temporary or minimal built start as part of the development process. Yardhouse (2014), the new, purpose-built workspace at Sugarhouse Studios in London, is temporary in the sense that it will only be in its current location for another two years. But we are using it as an argument for wider provision of affordable workspace on interim use sites and, specifically, to stitch space for making back into an idea of what an area under development needs.

To address the second half of your question: we are not set on a trajectory to win ever bigger and bigger work. Of course, working at different scales offers amazing opportunities, and large projects – which mean more of us can work together, develop new ideas and learn more – have a really powerful appeal. But it's not the same as increasing the quantity of work. What matters to us is the way of working, our relationship to the output, and really being able to commit to what we are doing.

What advice would you give to a young student looking to make the same route into architecture and set up their own practice?

AD: Find a team.

FIGURE 4.10: above / Yardhouse is an affordable workspace building in Sugarhouse Yard and a pilot for the provision of creative workspaces, completed in 2014

INTERVIEW 08 /
EXYZT

NICHOLAS
HENNINGER

Born in 2003 on the initiative of five architects, EXYZT is now a multidisciplinary creative platform bringing together more than 20 people: architects, graphic designers, videographers, photographers, DJs, botanists and manufacturers. It aims to challenge the view of architecture as an independent field of practice, and to embark instead on experimental living ventures built collectively. Each project, often taking the form of a temporary installation, is seen as a 'playground' in which cultural behaviours and shared stories relate, mix and mingle. For the 10th Venice Architecture Biennale in 2006, EXYZT transformed the French pavilion into a place of encounter and exchange, with a real kitchen, hotel, sauna and mini-pool on the roof.

How did you start EXYZT?

Nicholas Henninger: We started EXYZT after graduating from Paris-La Villette (ENSAPLV) in 2003. Usually at the end of school you're designing personal projects, which you develop on the basis of an idea, a site, a concept; we didn't want to do separate projects, the five of us wanted to practice together.

We took over a patch of land in the centre of Paris. We decided that the basic programme was just to inhabit the space and take it from there; to understand the place, to engage our bodies with the urban environment physically and to generate new encounters by opening the doors of our (public) house – that's what I liked when I learnt that a pub was a public house, someone opens up his place, there are these blurry boundaries between public and private.

We came up with this idea EXYZT because X, Y and Z are the three coordinates of space, T is time and E is energy, that's the basic framework of making a space; making architecture requires the energy and the time to project it into 3D.

How much of your work would you say is temporary?

NH: Well, EXYZT is mostly a project, not a studio. For the past 10 years it's been a collective project: everyone has been sharing ideas and we've all been living in different cities. The idea was to really experiment through temporary projects and, at the same time, test real set-ups, for example on a plot of land with disused buildings.

All our projects have been temporary but some of them have been pioneering in the ways that they have been used afterwards that we didn't expect initially. Our projects also help others access sites across the city. We're still on the site of the Southwark Lido, for example; it created some confidence with the landlords and now I'm working on different things for them.

FIGURE 4.11: previous / Southwark Lido in 2008
FIGURE 4.12: above / EXYZT, made up of artists, architects, photographers and filmmakers, come together from different locations to organise 'experimental living ventures' and to inhabit a project completely

FIGURE 4.13: above / each of EXYZT's projects is seen as a 'playground' for cultural engagement, inviting local communities and the public to appropriate the spaces, Southwark Lido, 2008

Back in 2008, how did the Southwark Lido in London come about, and what was the idea behind that project?

NH: It was an invitation from the Architecture Foundation to create inhabited architecture for the 2008 London Festival of Architecture. We saw this land and thought it was a nice space – by the railway, with the viaduct at the back and the trains passing by – you're really in the city here. It's also well orientated, south-facing; it was land awaiting redevelopment and we could see how our collective could take over this space. Sometimes through discussions we like to pick up elements of the culture or the country we're coming into, so the Lido was something everyone could understand. It also involves water in the public space; water is an element we've been working a lot with because it's something that's very engaging for people – it's playful and performative.

What was it like working with the filmmaker Sara Muzio on the project? Were there any challenges to collaborating?

NH: No, not at all. She was part of the collective and she was my girlfriend, actually! We met when we did the French Pavilion at the 2006 Venice Architecture Biennale. Sarah Ichioka was working with the curator, Ricky Burdett, at the time, so that's how we met the guys at the Architecture Foundation for the Southwark Lido.

Sara Muzio is a filmmaker, and also has a background in architecture. As we work as a collective, it's about bringing all these skills together: everyone who works on these projects has different goals, so our aim is to capture life using different mediums. The collective is basically a residency that we open to others. Each project acts as a place for a residency to occur, for example, where you invite a photographer to work with the neighbourhood, filmmakers to capture the life and builders to test different things. So, each project is not only about creating a piece of architecture, it's also about inhabiting it, using the situation to work and find your medium of expression.

How long was the Southwark Lido there for?

NH: It was probably one of our shortest projects, but it was really intense. The interesting thing about temporary projects is that they involve very intense energy in a very short amount of time. There was not so much temporary or pop-up architecture at the time – it's quite a recent thing and now suddenly all these young collectives have come along!

Do you think it was sparked by the Southwark Lido or your work in any way?

NH: Certainly our project opened possibilities. It's funny: nowadays people in various organisations still remember this project, because it helped a lot of different organisations or young architects or people on the council to see what temporary projects can look like. It created confidence – I think that's important. It's not looking at this project as a piece in itself; it helped contribute by breaking the ice a bit. It's funny because Maria from Assemble helped as a student, and Paloma and Lettice from Practice Architecture did too.

After the Lido, we fast-forward to 2012 when you did The Reunion on the same site. How did that happen and how did the site evolve?

NH: Basically, two years after the Lido happened, the Architecture Foundation for the next London Festival of Architecture, in 2010, commissioned Wayward Plants to create the Union Street Urban Orchard. Then it was 2012 and Roger Zogolovitch called us and said, 'The site's still there. Shouldn't we do something for the Olympic year?' We were happy to think about something. We had never returned to a site after doing a temporary project before.

We brought back the paddling pools – we wanted to create a big set-up for the neighbourhood as a more summery place. We didn't just have the empty land; there were some empty arches, so we thought it would be a good idea to invest in these spaces as well. Before they started to rebuild the new block of flats next door, there was a really nice garden with hollyhocks and flowers. What we created was essentially all the elements of a public house – getting people together, games, and we also had some sleeping pods, a sauna and some South London brewed beers being sold from under one arch.

It stayed open for two months, so we invited people to propose activities here – a yoga course, for example, or painting workshops at the back of the arches. We programmed some of it ourselves in advance – some performances, some screenings – but then we left a lot of room for people just to turn up. This time we met much more with our neighbours because last time, for the Southwark Lido, was a bit too short. When they knew that we were coming back with a new project they were really happy about that.

Since then we've been building up some interesting relationships with the neighbours, even if it's difficult to get people involved on a regular basis. But we share the space with them and that's what I'm looking at – to reopen the space as a garden, maybe hosting some little food businesses during the summer, and bringing back a little paddling pool because I know most of the kids in the area are just waiting for that!

Now you have the site until 2016, what are you planning?

NH: For the site, I'm going to do some workshops with some students and I'm teaching at Central Saint Martins to create a tea pavilion. It's going to grow organically. Why I've got the site until 2016 is because the original scheme for this site has been replaced with a different scheme with housing. Zogolovitch already had the planning consent for one development but he wanted to see if there could be some crossover with the development of the arches by Network Rail, so he gave himself another two years to see if there could be some kind of mutual development. He's been working on a new small flat development called Solidspace, so he wants to create a full mock-up of one of the flats on the site. I've also been in touch with some neighbours to maybe create a brewery/laboratory here.

We also have a structure here by Rural Studio. Rural Studio has been working a lot on creating low-cost houses in Austin, Texas. It's all about making and learning through making. They had been doing research into using timber from thinning in the forest – the process of cutting non-mature trees to let others mature – and they created this pavilion that is on the site now. It was in the V&A exhibition 1:1 Architects Build Small Spaces (2010). It now belongs to Roger

FIGURE 4.14: above / The Reunion returned to the Southwark Lido site with a playful outdoor space, complete with paddling pools and handmade wooden furniture in 2013

Zogolovitch, the landlord, and for four years it was in storage. I would like it to become a bit more like a public space where you can hang out. I'm looking at this concept of a convenience room – if you're a neighbour and you need a little gallery, you can use it, or if you want to make a meeting or a meal between neighbours.

What does the future hold for you? Are you going to continue doing these sorts of projects?

NH: We're going to change our status from a collective to a platform. Over the years we've been doing it, we were all always doing lots of different things and EXYZT was something we would get together once or twice a year for. As one of the founders, it is the core of my practice, but now I tend to evolve through this kind of

approach, learning from the making. We just won a really interesting project with muf architecture/art in Croydon: it's not specifically architecture, but we're designing strategies towards spacing people – the core of the project is based around social and economic activities. Rather than saying 'We want a school, we want to talk about education,' or, 'We're doing housing, a shop,' it's more about how they connect people to their city.

We're also doing a website where you can follow all the people who have collaborated with us. We're not working alone as a brand or as a company; we're always in touch with other practices and it's been interesting to exchange ideas. It's a community of different practices, like Assemble and Raumlabor. You can also see that in different countries people are trying different things. Some projects are more in line with the

FIGURE 4.15: above / The Reunion used one of the railway arches to create a bar and sell locally brewed beer, inspired by the traditional British pub

FIGURE 4.16: above / The Reunion utilised a wild neighbouring garden before a new block of flats was built on it

traditional production of architecture, but for me, personally, it's really the aspect of 'design and build' that I'm interested in. I want to reclaim this term, which frightens every architect because it makes them think a company's going to take over the project, doing it cheaply, without any consideration to detailing. Whereas for me, it's the essential basis: the designing and the building. That's why I'm more interested in looking at smaller-scale projects, where construction and design can also integrate young people.

What impact do you think these temporary structures can have on the architecture profession in general?

NH: I think they create some hope for students. They can see that you can reopen the scope of architectural practice, that it's not only 'We're doing all these studies and then we start work in an office being a CAD monkey.' It offers more possibilities to a young generation who come out of the school – being able to be touched by such practice, or being informed by such practice, shows that some other direction can be possible. On the temporary aspect of things, I think that this kind of practice is a real tool to be able to test the ground, test ideas and test the occupation of a space. When we did the Dalston Mill, for example, the fact that I had done temporary projects before and then was involved in the long term helped my ideas be clearer in terms of occupying the space – what was essential to ensure this project worked with the existing space.

Temporary projects focus on the human scale, rather than the big infrastructure of a building. When we create new places, like Stratford for example, and when you're a local, little trader, you don't have any opportunity to take part in a big development because of the scale. It's only the big brands that can afford to invest money first.

But there are lots of people out there with amazing ideas, and we can say, 'OK, we can start small and you can begin to craft your own activity.' You can challenge even building regulations with simple detailing, and you can create things with a limited amount of resources, which don't cost too much but that can support a lot of businesses. You get a better idea of what is essential.

What advice would you give to students wishing to take a similar route into architecture?

NH: Just go out there. Especially in a city like London, in every corner you've got organisations dealing with different issues in the city. Just get involved, meet people, look outside, don't wait in your office. If you don't go out there, you can't understand. There are plenty of opportunities to do small projects, little pavilions, or even helping someone to build something. That doesn't mean you don't need your architecture skills and education to organise all that but it's very interesting how I started to learn about London, about architecture in England, by doing these temporary projects. That's why at some point, after the Dalston Mill in 2009, I said, 'This city is great!' I could feel something because I was out there – I met lots of people, different types of people, young and old. That's when you can start to activate conversations and understand environments.

It's just about going out there and finding opportunities. Find a small patch of land, find out who the landlord is, convince him to create a garden first and then things can grow from there. Be proactive, and don't be afraid to get your hands dirty.

FIGURE 4.17: above top / Dalston Mill turned a disused railway line and waste ground into a vibrant rural retreat in 2009
FIGURE 4.18: above bottom / visitors could drop in to use the baking ovens or participate in one of the events or workshops

INTERVIEW 09 /
PRACTICE ARCHITECTURE

LETTICE DRAKE /
PALOMA GORMLEY /
HENRY STRINGER

Practice Architecture is a London-based design and build practice founded in 2009 by Lettice Drake, Paloma Gormley and Henry Stringer. Past projects include The Yard Theatre in Hackney Wick, Frank's Cafe on the top of a multi-storey car park in Peckham, a straw bale auditorium for Bold Tendencies, and the founding of a community workspace with the Architecture Foundation in South Kilburn. Consistent in its work has been its involvement in each stage of a project, from inception through to construction. It builds its buildings itself, working with teams of friends and volunteers who, like Practice Architecture, often learn on the job. This construction principle shapes the design process, using low-tech materials with straightforward construction techniques to create buildings with a strong internal logic – and which can be made by a relatively unskilled work force.

How did you meet and start Practice Architecture?

Lettice Drake /Paloma Gormley: We never intended to set up a practice. Our first project happened in 2009, straight out of university, after which we were approached by other people to get involved in new things. One project rolled into another and a few years later we thought it might be good to come up with a name. We work in a very informal way, we are not fully qualified architects, we have never had a formal contract, or been personally or professionally insured. We have always worked in relationships of trust and mutual responsibility – an increasingly risky thing to do in a highly litigious culture. Apart from electricians we don't employ contractors but build everything ourselves with friends, lovers, family, students, volunteers and passersby. Every project has been different, exposed us to new things and been an opportunity to learn. Our name is an expression of this, but there's no end game or idea of an ultimate recital; we see our work as a continual process of learning. As such, we will continue to practice living and making for the rest of our lives.

We are continually working right up to the limit of our experience and capacity, which means we spend a lot of time inventing processes rather than drawing from any experience of common practice. While this perhaps means we aren't limited by a prescriptive understanding of convention, it also means we don't have the benefits of accumulated wisdom and have to make all the mistakes ourselves. In response, we've become good at asking lots of questions.

We make decisions together with our clients and collaborators and are accountable for them together – meaning we take a direct collective and personal responsibility for our actions and for what we produce. We don't feel a service provider/client distinction – we are a group of people making something happen.

Did you set out to create temporary structures or did things just happen that way?

LD/PG: Most of the projects we have worked on began as temporary because that was the only way they could be instigated. There is a lot more space for risk in temporary projects; they offer a place to experiment and to be inexperienced. Short-life projects can be a great way to test an idea that can then grow in strength, demonstrate itself, and potentially evolve into something more permanent. It can also help broker an initial cheap lease that can make a longer-term project viable by enabling it to take root in the first place.

Over the years, our ideas about what the space of impermanence means have gone through quite a shift. We have an increasing desire to make things that are solid, embedded, invested – that have longevity and that represent an investment in and expression of a geographical community. While 'temporary' allows for risk, experimentation and playfulness increasingly feels synonymous with 'vulnerable'. We've become increasingly aware of the role of narrative and that, without really realising it, narrative has been one of the most active threads in our work. This lack of awareness has meant that at points we have been involved in the creation of stories that we didn't want to tell. Temporary architecture is porous, legible, quick, cheap and exciting to look at, as it seems to challenge the order of things. It is often public – creating sites of interaction and exchange where we make displays of togetherness.

The narrative power of temporary architecture has been quickly recognised by the key-holding powers of the city. Large businesses, institutions, local authorities and developers have all adopted the pop-up as a form of real life three-dimensional rendering, for creating fantasy images of community, opulence or earthiness. In such projects there is an end in mind beyond that of the immediate experience: it's a means to raise the 'cultural' profile of an area (thus attracting developers and wealthier residents), or to boost a brand or sell a product. They are marketing exercises. The images created are very powerful and travel much further than any individual's experience.

FIGURE 4.19: previous / The Yard Theatre in London was designed to be entirely adaptable and constantly changing to accommodate each performance, 2011
FIGURE 4.20: above / a small raised amphitheatre created for a sculpture park at Roche Court in Wiltshire in 2010

FIGURE 4.21: above / the structure of Frank's Cafe was made for Bold Tendencies, a very young Peckham-based organisation, to accompany their summer sculpture exhibition

I understand that you worked on EXYZT's Southwark Lido. What was that experience like and what did you learn from it?

LD/PG: It was amazing watching EXYZT work. There was a seamlessness to their collaborations that held the construction work, social engagement, sign printing and site-made pasta in total equilibrium. EXYZT's projects are temporary in an active and provocative way. Each one is a different proposal of how we might live, work, exchange and interact with each other. They always work on their own terms. While the projects may be temporary, taking place across the world, for the collective they become a permanent way of life: they move from one city to another and live on site throughout, hosting and activating each space and inviting everyone to join to them. Our practice is more conventional. While we have been very involved in the instigation, design and construction of each project, once it is complete we generally take a step back. Helping out on the Lido had a big impact on us in terms of defining the scope of what felt possible. It was an incredibly open and generous environment, and a very inspiring way of working. We feel very lucky to have been able to help and to learn from their projects and continue to share thoughts and ideas. They have remained good friends ever since.

How did the project for Frank's Cafe in Peckham come about, and what were some of the ideas behind it?

LD/PG: We were approached by Bold Tendencies, a very young Peckham-based

FIGURE 4.22: above / looking over the city from the top of the Peckham car park

organisation, to think about making a café to accompany their summer sculpture exhibition. We went and visited the car park on a freezing afternoon in October. It was an incredibly dramatic and unusual space – urban, yet with a view and sense of removal you associate with a park. You are profoundly in the city, surrounded by it on all sides in the form of a 360-degree panorama that takes in every iconic building in London. The idea of building something in that context was thrilling and daunting in equal measure.

The main pragmatic concern was making sure the thing wouldn't blow off. The final solution was these giant ratchet straps that would lash the structure to the roof, forming a loop over and under the deck and ensuring the café couldn't take off, while simultaneously creating supports

for the roof, which would slide out along the red ribbons of webbing. The straps are the first signal of the café's presence as you pass under them on the lower deck. Spatially we were interested in how you could construct something that was informal and contained different moments of intimacy: nooks to snuggle into, shelves to clamber onto, and long narrow tables where you'd be thrown together with strangers.

The materials we used were readily available and cheap – we used scaffolding planks for almost everything, bolting them together to make the heavier structural elements. We found a company that fabricated drop-down sides for lorries to fabricate the oversized ratchet straps and red PVC roof. That first year the whole thing was built for under £5,000.

Initially we were going to design, build and run the café, but we gradually realised that alongside our other commitments this wasn't going to be possible and we got Frank on board. Over the following years we continued to work on other projects in the car park, introducing other bits of infrastructure: different kinds of seating, structures for displaying information, bike stands, market tables and lamps, and a large straw auditorium we built on the lower floor.

FIGURE 4.23: left / old scaffolding planks were used to create both the roof structure of Frank's Cafe and the café furniture

FIGURE 4.24: above / preparing to hoist up the red PVC roof of the cafe

FIGURE 4.25: above/ Practice Architecture's risk assessment and site safety

What was the construction process like?

LD/PG: Part of our methodology is to design things in a way that they can be made by anyone. Initially, this was practically motivated as none of us really had any experience of building anything, but over time it has also developed into a language – the buildings and structures describe and celebrate their means of construction.

There was a fearless energy around at that time, with many other projects happening in the building and surrounding area and a collective sense that a lot was possible. The car park was this playground, lawless and full of people making, building, trying things out, helping each other, teaching each other, falling in love and working through the night. The build began with 300 scaffolding boards that arrived at the bottom of the car park and which we slowly moved to the top on the roof of an old Volvo. Then we began working out how to put them together with a £10 Tesco skill saw and a few cordless drills. People turned up to help and things picked up pace. A friend designed some very simple scaffolding plank trestle tables, and we developed minimal screw methods for making bar stools, chairs and benches by mucking around with bits of wood on site and seeing what stood up. Getting the roof on was a big operation. We assembled everyone on the top deck and tugged, teased, hauled and cranked the roof into position, and raised the central columns of the structure that put the straps under the last bit of tension – and suddenly there was this space and everything was bathed in a deep red glow. It was a very happy and exhausting three weeks.

FIGURE 4.26: above / scaffolding planks were bolted together to create the main structural elements of the rooftop café

You develop quite a particular relationship with a structure when you are building it yourself and you're part-living on site – you become completely immersed in the life that is the creation of that project. So when it opens to the public it can be quite hard to make that shift.

You are often working right up until the last minute, haven't been home for days and then suddenly someone you have never met is casually rolling a cigarette while chatting to their friends on the bench that was, but is no longer, your bed. Every bit of the building is embedded with some memory of who made it, what a nightmare it was to get those bolts in, whose blood it is staining the bar… These memories are intimate, close up, and then you watch the place that made them being experienced in a completely different way.

What impact do you think Frank's Cafe has had on Peckham? Perhaps the project has also had an impact on the temporary architecture movement too?

LD/PG: That's a huge question and one that we are struggling with all the time. The social potential of space is what motivates us to construct new spaces – and, as a social space, Frank's Cafe is not at all what we had imagined. This is partly to do with its popular success, necessitating a different scale and kind of operation, partly due to a lack of foresight and coherence among those who made it happen, and partly because of the way it was communicated and who to. In hindsight we would have approached the project quite differently as we increasingly understand the extent to which the success of any project lies in the soft architecture of the organisation, as much as or more than the hard architecture of a building. The two things need to be in synthesis. The real impact of Frank's Cafe on Peckham has come more from what the café represented as an 'event' than from what it offers as a space. Alongside the many arts projects happening in the area it attracted a lot of media

FIGURE 4.27: above / Frank's Cafe is a temporary summer bar on the roof of a multi-storey car park in Peckham, first installed in 2009

attention, broadcasting Peckham to new audiences and contributing to a shifting demographic and rapidly increasing property prices. Many arts spaces in Peckham have now closed or are rehousing themselves further out of London and the buildings are being re-populated with more bars and cafés. We hear a lot about artist communities that are affected by gentrification and which are seen, to some extent, as victims of the Pied Piper power of their own activities.

What we don't hear so much about are the many other individuals, families and communities that are also displaced in the process. The project has made us think long and hard about the impact of projects of this kind – who they are for and what they promote. We bear an uneasy sense of responsibility for elements of its impact, though the project may have helped to save the car park

from demolition and development. It is an incredible publically owned building and as such should be accessible to everyone. In terms of its impact on the temporary architecture movement it's hard to say. When we first built Frank's we'd never heard the term 'pop-up', which is hard to imagine now as it has become so familiar. The café and sculpture exhibition became a very public and accessible demonstration that young people can have an impact on the city and can make their own place in it, but this kind of thing had been happening for decades in squats and warehouses across the country. Frank's really appeared towards the end of what was in retrospect a particularly creative, concentrated, chaotic and free time for young artists in Peckham, enabled by its invisibility, the availability of space, and affordable rents.

FIGURE 4.28: above / like Frank's Cafe, the Yard Theatre in London was made with old scaffolding boards

How did the project for The Yard Theatre (2011) come about, and what were some of the ideas behind that?

LD/PG: Jay [Miller], the director who founded The Yard, wanted to create a dedicated theatre where young writers, actors and directors could develop and show experimental work on their own terms. Initially, he was keen to make a space that was entirely adaptable and constantly changing to accommodate each show. We were excited by the idea of a Fun Palace-esque space but were aware that in attempting to accommodate everything you can end up facilitating lots of things badly.

The theatre is configured with a thrust stage and seats 110 at maximum capacity. It is small and very intimate, with the audience nearly falling onto the stage. There is something reassuring in the experience of using a traditional typology rather than always trying to reinvent the wheel. The previous year we had built a small raised timber amphitheatre for a sculpture park in Salisbury. It's a small structure, yet it can seat 70 people. There was something powerful in the closeness and focus it created that definitely informed the way we approached The Yard.

The theatre was built inside a large industrial shed in Hackney Wick. The rake of the seating created an acoustic and fire-separating wall between the theatre and bar – allowing those two functions to cohabit, the one sliding over the other. Under the theatre's belly we nestled dimly lit low tables and benches. We essentially adapted the same system of scaffolding boards as we had used in Frank's and the amphitheatre to build the primary structure. Discarded lino from the media centre of the Olympics, passed on to us by Assemble, created the acoustic lining for the walls; old chairs

with their legs cut off created the bank of seats; and the strip lights we had removed from the building while making South Kilburn Studios were incorporated into the bar. The material choices were really governed by what was accessible to us, as the budget for the project was £7,000. Dusty pink polyfilled fire-rated plasterboard lined the cantilevered external wall, thrusting into the bar. The dressing room is contained within the bar and it has translucent walls to display the silhouettes of the performers as they prepare for each show.

Seeing as many of your projects are temporary, what happens to your projects afterwards? Do some stay longer than they are first intended or do some get recycled for example?

LD/PG: None of the projects we have made were meant to last more than three months and it is only in contributing to this book that we have realised that every one has somehow survived, some up to six years later, which is quite a testimony to the power and durability of temporariness.

What does the future hold for Practice Architecture? Will you continue to design temporary structures?

LD/PG: We are currently working on our first building that will have floors and walls and roof and has to stay warm and dry! It's a studio/house in London. It takes a lot of lessons from our past projects, and we are working in a very similar way but on a different time frame and scale. It is a simple bolted system of Douglas fir boards that creates a three-storey solid timber frame which will be in-filled with a mixture of hemp shiv and lime. The project was designed to be built quickly and cheaply; we had initially imagined it taking six months but are coming to realise that permanent buildings require a little more attention to detail!

What advice would you give to a young student looking to follow the same route into architecture and set up their own practice?

LD/PG: Perhaps what has enabled us to begin to work in the way we have was time and space, both of which are increasingly a luxury as the cost of living and property rises. When we started building things we were at an age and in a position where it felt like a lot of people around us had the time and energy to make things happen. Perhaps we wouldn't have been able to do so much if we'd started with the intention of setting up an architecture practice, which immediately conjures images of a fixed workplace, filing systems, contracts and salaries – things which might have distracted us and made us more apprehensive about just getting on with it. The projects have all been, in their different manifestations, attempts to make places for a shared culture to be explored – to make places of production, coming together and play. What has defined that experience has been working with our peers, taking risks and continuing to dream a bit, believing that things are possible and you don't have to accept the territory you are given.

FIGURE 4.29: above / discarded lino from the media centre of the Olympics, passed on by Assemble, was used to line the walls of the theatre

PERSPECTIVE /
BUILDING ALTERNATIVE POSSIBLE WORLDS

MARIANA PESTANA

Under the all-encompassing term 'temporary architecture' lies a mixed landscape of projects and practices that vary in their methodologies, processes and outcomes. Usually consisting of some kind of spatial structure activated by a programme of events, temporary architectures swiftly appear to disappear: durational by definition, they contrast with the urban landscape of permanent architectures where they pop up. I have long been interested in the kind of temporary architecture that responds to, disrupts and reimagines the places and contexts in which it emerges. In depicting possibilities, imagining scenarios and testing situations lies the value of a kind of practice engaged with designing 'alternative possible worlds'.

THIS IS TEMPORARY

Let me explain what I mean by this. As we all know, architecture repeats itself through systems, programmes and typologies, which we have become accustomed to considering 'normal'. Architect and critic Sam Jacob has explained this very well: as architecture becomes part of the landscape of the everyday, its banality confers reality upon it.[3] As he argues, architecture repeats materiality (think of bricks) and structural systems (think of grids), but also typologies and programmes, and this constant repetition is a form of making it seem 'natural'. The problem that this 'normality' entails is, in my opinion, the fact that it perpetuates ideologies that determine the ways in which architecture is made and – most importantly – used.

Disguised as 'normal', architecture materialises power structures and choreographs behaviours and relationships of authority that we often forget to question. The durational quality of temporary architecture opens up opportunities to create spaces which break through the 'normality' of the everyday landscape, and propose alternatives. In the temporality of such work – often regarded as its main fragility – lies a disruptive trigger, one that can generate, for a moment in time, alternative, non-actual possibilities. It's as if the brief lifespan of temporary architecture offers a glimpse of something other than the reality of the everyday.

When in 2009 I visited the Dalston Mill[4] to interview the authors of the project, EXYZT, and instinctively called it a fiction, I got a straightforward answer: 'A fiction? But it's here, it's built, it's real!' It was no fiction, according to the authors, because they had made it real. It is true that in architecture the terms reality and fiction are often seen through binary lens, usually grounded in an antagonist distinction between what is built and what is not.[5] But happily – and in contrast with the rigidity with which the distinction between the two terms is made in the field of architectural design – literary theory provides flexible, malleable and interdependent definitions of reality and fiction. By translating such flexibility into the field of architecture, perhaps we can acknowledge the interstitial space, neither entirely real nor entirely fictional, that particular works of temporary architecture create.

Many authors have constructed, in their literary works, alternative worlds to the one in which we live. The study of such worlds has been the subject of several works of literary theory, and in the literary field, the notion of possible worlds is different from the philosophical concept of the same name. In the literary possible worlds theory, fiction is described as a gesture of recentring, where the author becomes a 'citizen' of the world of the text and invites the reader to follow him, thus establishing a 'fictional pact' with the reader and allowing him to be a 'temporary member' of the recentred system that the text provides.[6]

This metaphor of citizenship lends itself quite well to the discussion that is at place here: we could say that in materialising 'what if' scenarios, a work of temporary architecture invites users to become temporary members of its system. Authors of such works could be said to establish fictional pacts with users, granting them citizenship in an alternative world made possible only for a moment in time. Whether readers (in literature) or users (in architecture), citizens of the new system of reality get to know a world other than the one in which they move every day.

It is generally known that the worlds created by works of literary fiction have the potential to problematise what we consider evident in the actual world. They can make us reconsider it and reset our views, review our beliefs or behaviour.[7] I wish to argue that, in a similar way, worlds created by 'temporary architecture' constitute empowering hypotheses and tests available for users to explore, and that in doing so they engage with what anthropologist Arjun Appadurai has called a politics of possibility: 'I mean those ways of thinking, feeling and acting that increase the horizons of hope, that expand the field of the imagination, that produce greater equity in what I have called the capacity to aspire, and that widen the field of informed, creative and critical citizenship.'[8]

By adding fictional layers to the normality of the everyday, temporary architecture has the potential to distribute imaginative power, raise critical awareness and foment desire for a world otherwise. In its tenuous brevity and despite the fragility of its existence, temporary architecture holds an immense potential: not only does it make us aware of the real, but it also reminds us that reality can be changed. It's time we recognised its place within architectural practice and discourse.

CHAPTER 05 /
PARTICIPATIVE BUILDING AND MATERIALITY: SCARCITY OF RESOURCES AND A PLATFORM FOR COMMUNICATION

INTERVIEWS:
FOLKE KÖBBERLING AND MARTIN KALTWASSER [GERMANY] / PLASTIQUE FANTASTIQUE [GERMANY]

When a structure is only around for a short amount of time, what it's made of and how it's made can become incredibly important. One-off installations can initially seem like a waste of resources, and the consideration of what's going to happen to the materials afterwards all too often an afterthought. But, as the saying goes, one man's trash is another man's treasure: from scrap material and found objects to blow-up bubbles formed in a matter of minutes, this chapter looks at how two practices are using materials to gather and empower people to think about sustainable, self-initiated ways of building.

[145]

Interviewed in this chapter, Berlin-based artist duo Folke Köbberling and Martin Kaltwasser, in their own idiosyncratic way use throwaway objects and discarded materials, found and collected themselves, to create ad hoc, self-built urban interventions. Using very few resources – a hodgepodge of timber pallets, bulky refuse, hand-me-down stage sets and junk picked off the street, obtained from local building sites or donated by friends and neighbours – these improvised, site-specific projects comment on issues ranging from consumption and grass-roots participation to sustainability and the scarcity of resources. Often assembled by a close-knit team of volunteers and students, on derelict urban sites and the last few remaining gaps in the city with unrestricted access, they're examples of empowerment – a call to action for collaborative, collective, participatory design. Against a backdrop of the privatisation of public space and surveillance, these impromptu structures also share a social concern for facilitating spontaneous encounters in urban public spaces. In their 2009 book *Hold It!*, Köbberling and Kaltwasser comment: 'Our projects seek to challenge conventional and tendentiously backward-looking approaches in planning and building, conditioned by social segregation, and formally executed in an architectural language that idealises historical precedence. Using a build-it-yourself approach to set up constructions and buildings made from found surplus and reject materials, we are positing alternatives in experimental, open and communicative urban planning strategies that transcend familiar eurocentrist and historical concepts.'

Their projects take on a form of their own, shaped by the back-to-basics building process. As they explain in the interview, with little, if any, fixed technical drawings or models to guide them, structures are literally made up as they go along, often dependent on what materials are available to hand. 'We always go with the material,' Köbberling says. 'We never create models because we don't know what the thing will look like. You can shape it a little but you never know how a façade will look until you're there. A lot of people don't like that process because it's so situationalist, a little bit chaotic and much more time consuming.' Adds Kaltwasser: 'After having completed the basic structure we make the

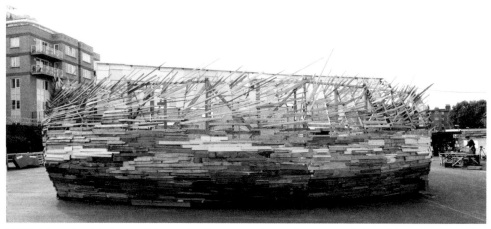

FIGURE 5.1: previous / the Emotion Maker, an inflatable structure by Plastique Fantastique at Clerkenwell Design Week in 2011
FIGURE 5.2: above / the Jellyfish Theatre by Folke Köbberling and Martin Kaltwasser was a temporary theatre created on a school playground in Southwark for the Oikos Theatre Festival in 2010

cladding, the building of walls, doors and interior design from found material. In this stage of building we act very freely, very sculptural.'

The Jellyfish Theatre, for example, was a squat, spaceship-like temporary theatre created on a school playground in Southwark over one summer for the Oikos Project and the London Festival of Architecture in 2010. Built by more than 100 volunteers, it was the first theatre building in London made completely from scrap material. The 120-seat construction, made of discarded theatre sets and hundreds of humble timber pallets sourced from New Covent Garden market, hosted a series of climate change-based plays drawn up by The Red Room Theatre Company. Without any electricity on site, uncut pallets, sheets of wood and old doors were hammered haphazardly by hand onto a steel structural frame, gaining a life of their own and seemingly exploding out behind the dressing rooms to form the 'tentacles'. 'The bankers and businessmen passed by our stone-age site construction site and they could feel and smell that we were the nicest, best, most enthusiastic and funniest construction site in the whole of London!' enthuses Kaltwasser.

Another project, Amphis, is an octagonal, two-storey theatre, also made of discarded materials, created in just six weeks by 40 volunteers on the site of Wysing Arts Centre in Cambridgeshire in 2008. The 6m-tall structure was built on a falsework made from pallets and timber beams, filled with compressed sand and rubble because concrete was too expensive.

FIGURE 5.3: above / the Amphis Theatre coming together, with the help of 40 volunteers

Rejected material, including teak, came from nearby Cambridge University, while the large central timber-panel ground floor had previously served as a stage dance floor. Its black lino surround was made from discarded college worktops. Says Kaltwasser: 'As soon as we start a construction, we communicate a lot with passersby and visitors, and then a snowball effect starts. After a short time, everybody knows we need material and sometimes we are literally overflooded with free building material.' Now that it has become a favoured refuge of local birds of prey, due to several openings that cannot be shut, the structure still stands, five years after it was supposed to be dismantled. 'The thing with temporary structures is that you can experiment more and then you think, "Yes, this is really working, let it stand there",' says Köbberling.

However, Köbberling and Kaltwasser reveal in the interview that they are finding it increasingly difficult to create these ad hoc structures due to more and more rules and regulations putting constraints on experimentation and improvised designs. There are very few sites in our cities now that can be built on at a whim, without permissions or planning consents; the architect or designer has less opportunity to work autonomously, but often needs to involve the city, municipal controls, institutions and organisations. Overly cautious health and safety nets also mean that projects need to be thoroughly planned and vetted before they are built. Indeed, it is interesting that Köbberling and Kaltwasser are now going their separate ways, because for Köbberling: 'The freedom of creating is missing and then you are totally into architecture. You cannot work with the material any more. If you

FIGURE 5.4: above / inside the Emotion Maker by Plastique Fantastique, the stark white bubble created a reflective, intimate experience

don't like something, you cannot just exchange it.' Plastique Fantastique, meanwhile, has made its name by sticking religiously to just one building material – polyethylene, otherwise known as plastic. Its approach was first developed when founder Marco Canevacci was faced with the task of heating an empty factory he had rented in Berlin. 'It's quite a cheap material; you can easily seal it and create these kind of basic bubbles,' explains Canevacci in the interview. 'We filled it with warm air and that was it. They were the first rooms we produced, in 1999. That was the beginning, and afterwards I realised the potential of designing these kind of architectures. I think there's something magical about a structure popping up in 20 minutes and at the same time disappearing as fast as it inflates itself.'

It's the immediacy that excites Canevacci: 'I'm interested in this because standard architecture takes a really long time to express yourself and after a couple of years you might have something different in your mind.' These inflatable or pneumatic structures play with the potential of urban context, augmenting our perception of the city and animating the senses by squeezing themselves into narrow streets or inside buildings. Seemingly space-age and slightly alien in nature, they also play with transparency, fluidity, surfaces and layers. At the same time, they demand interaction and engagement from their users. 'Most of our installations are quite playful works [which] creates a communicative environment at once. It's a public thing, because people who don't know each other start to interact, communicate and interchange the experience you may have in this context,' says Canevacci.

FIGURE 5.5: above / Aeropolis, a project for the Metropolis Festival 2013 in Copenhagen, took one pneumatic structure around 13 different locations in the city

THIS IS TEMPORARY

The Emotion Maker at London's Clerkenwell Design Week in 2011, for example – a collaboration between Plastique Fantastique, sound designer Lorenzo Brusci and musician Marco Barotti – created a temporary performance chamber that housed an all-consuming, interactive sound installation. Participants were able to pick and choose from hundreds of music samples to create a composition of their own, while the stark white of the bubble created a reflective, intimate atmosphere that aimed to break down the formalised boundaries between people and their participation within a public space in the city. Says Canevacci: 'Only two people were allowed to enter the installation at one time, it took 10 minutes, and the experience inside was always a different one. It's funny because in most cases the two people didn't know each other.'

While that project placed the inflatable structure in an open public square, another project, Sound of Light (2014), pressed the bubble into the tight confines of an existing building, a 19th-century music pavilion in Hamm, Germany. 'If you take it as it is, it's just a geometric shape, but if you try to squeeze it into the existing environment it starts to change its shape and become something different, something you can apply to endless situations,' says Canevacci. Because the original pavilion in which it was constructed is relatively open, with two parallel rows of slender columns, the inflatable structure bulged out of all the gaps in between, giving the appearance of a rather strange silver worm ready to burst its seams. In just a few minutes, Plastique Fantastique had altered not only the existing architecture but the people's perception of that ordinarily open space, creating a totally new form and context. 'The structure is actually a tool to play with the urban landscape, so you use the bubble as a tool and then you have to add something on to it… like an installation,' explains Canevacci. In this case, Plastique Fantastique used a digital camera to transform sunlight into audio frequencies, effectively creating a 'giant vibrating loudspeaker'. Six hanging, coloured, inflatable 'columns' received the different frequencies from the sky above and converted the input from visible to audible via a series of woofers. By flooding the senses with colours, shapes, sounds and vibrations, Plastique Fantastique orchestrated a transitory dream-like experience, an altered reality transporting users to a new, never-experienced-before place.

At first glance, plastic might not seem like the most sustainable option. Yet, while temporary architecture raises serious concerns about reuse and recycling – often seen as quick, sporadic bursts of resources that are then quickly dismantled and thrown away – Plastique Fantastique's inflatable structures create endless possibilities for shapes, forms, and ultimately experiences, each new, spontaneous situation being entirely different from the one that went before. They can be reused time and time again to form a whole host of diverse, weird and wonderful urban interventions. Indeed, now Plastique Fantastique believes their potential can be more fully realised by focusing on placing these impromptu structures between existing buildings, narrow streets or squashed under highways, rather than the bubbles creating their own shapes in open spaces. 'You can place a bubble in a narrow street and it changes its shape and the street changes character as well. You don't have the street itself, you have something in between that is offering an experience or some weird shapes,' notes Canevacci. As such, it's about creating an open dialogue between users of the city and public space – a reinterpretation of the formal boundary between exterior and interior.

A project for the Metropolis Festival 2013 in Copenhagen, called Aeropolis, for instance, took one pneumatic structure around 13 different locations in the city. The same material adapted itself and changed shape depending on the location, from a silent disco at a noisy intersection of the city, to meditation and yoga sessions by a lake. These inflatable structures, dotted around our cities, could almost be seen as flash mobs, bringing people together when all too often we barely swap eye contact, let alone interact, on our urban streets.

Each practice, Folke Köbberling and Martin Kaltwasser, and Plastique Fantastique – incidentally both from Germany – use materiality in two unique ways to facilitate experimental, open and communicative design processes, empowering imaginative, spontaneous, new encounters in urban public spaces. Both invite audiences, especially students, to help during set-up, motivating and inspiring them to think about the city in alternative ways, while also using the structures as a platform, or indeed catalyser, for debate and free-flowing conversation between various participants during their short-lived manifestation. As Köbberling and Kaltwasser say: 'The built environment should be everyone's concern. Architects and artists could help to convey how to do things yourself, how to experiment and how to harness creative potential. This could be just the trigger.'

INTERVIEW 10 /
KÖBBERLING / KALTWASSER

MARTIN KALTWASSER /
FOLKE KÖBBERLING

Folke Köbberling and Martin Kaltwasser are an artist and architect duo based

in Berlin, Germany, who have been working together since the late 1990s. They

use discarded material and found objects to create projects in public spaces

that question issues such as our pressure to consume, growing surveillance and

the ever-increasing motor traffic that is threatening to change the appearance

of our cities in a fundamental way. They have lectured extensively in design

schools in Germany as well as the Emily Carr Institute of Art and Design

in Vancouver, the Art Center College of Design in Pasadena, the Technical

University of Vienna and Chelsea College of Art and Design in London. They

are now going their separate ways to concentrate on different interests.

How did you start working together and what made you decide to use throwaway objects and discarded materials in your projects?

Folke Köbberling: In 2002, a long time ago now, we were asked to do a lecture evening in the Volksbühne – a theatre on Rosa-Luxemburg-Platz in Berlin – and an exhibition on the informal housing in Istanbul. We did a lot of theoretical research and got really familiar with their construction techniques and the law, which comes from the Osmanian times, there, that you can build a house overnight. In Turkish it is called 'gecekondu' (from 'gece' meaning 'night' and 'condu' meaning 'house'). In the end we thought we would like to take this experience back to Berlin and see what the reaction would be like. We started to look for a space and found one in front of Gropiusstadt, a totally planned area in Berlin where 600,000 inhabitants live.

We thought it would be nice to build there and have all the surrounding high-rise buildings look down on us, like an annex almost, so that it would have a similar feeling to the housing in Istanbul. We looked on a construction site in the middle of Berlin for scrap material and beams. The size of the materials was the base for the construction. In the end we built a house overnight, with all its difficulties of lack of light and power. In former times, and still now, we use almost always scrap materials, even for our own homes – you just use what you can get in the street.

FIGURE 5.6: previous / the entrance to the Jellyfish Theatre
FIGURE 5.7: above / Hausbau was an entire family home built on a disused meadow overlooking a housing estate in 2004

What was the reaction to that first project?

FK: Everybody in the high-rises could see us building the house overnight and the reactions were very positive. The people living there had to walk past us every day and because we lived there with our two children, there was already a level of communication. We used this temporary structure to connect with people and talk about housing and sustainability. Were they alienated in their high-rises or would they like to have a house like we had there, even though it was only very temporary, even though it was only standing there for one week?

So in 2005 we planned it over a longer time and invited friends and students to do a bigger settlement. We looked and collected material for

three months, which we exhibited in an exhibition space before we started to build six individual buildings by six different architects and city planners. We wanted to see what would happen if nobody communicated with each other; it was an experiment in how city planning works if you don't talk, if you never have a meeting. It was really interesting because we all didn't really react to each other: everyone just looked for the best place, and in the end the settlement was very spread out.

Also, we wanted to get in contact again with the community of the Gropiusstadt. We were there the previous year and now we came to the site with many more people. So the barrier for the people of Gropiusstadt to cross was much higher than the year before. Afterwards we took the material down and brought all the scrap material to the

FIGURE 5.8: above / Hausbau was made of discarded timber found on Berlin's many building sites

FIGURE 5.9: above top / Musterhaus (Model House) was a one-family prefab home built in front of the Martin-Gropius-Bau museum in 2005

FIGURE 5.10: above bottom/material found for free throughout Zürich was sorted, stacked and displayed on the eighteen shelves of Köbberling and Kaltwasser's buildings materials centre

Martin-Gropius-Bau, a museum, where we built a project called the Musterhaus on the parking lot. Built on a green area of the Martin Gropius Bau premises in Berlin, the Musterhaus (Model House) is a one–family prefab model house. In its cube shape it rather resembles the T–Com House, a high-tech house, which a manufacturer of prefabricated houses had put on show in central Berlin to advertise the delights of suburban life.

In contrast to this, we made the Musterhaus from materials widely available on Berlin's streets, disused lots and building sites: bulky scrap, used materials, random finds and construction waste. The Musterhaus, just a stone's throw from Potsdamer Platz, formed a marked contrast to the Berlin monoculture of block buildings and the rigid plans for the city's urban development.

How easy is it to get hold of discarded materials for your temporary projects?

FK: I would say we really became experts in finding material. You look for materials in each city, on the street. If you also think about fairs and biennales, you already know there will be millions of booths, where people come, build something, and end up with 90% of the material in the trash. We really try to make the logistics transparent. We lectured at the Berlin University of the Arts in 2008 and tried to make an internet platform where the leftover material from installations and structures at fairs could be made available, free, for everybody. Unfortunately we did not have enough resources to make it work, but nowadays there are more platforms that specialise in scrap material.

In the UK we have websites such as Freecycle for domestic objects, but I wonder whether, like you say, there should be a similar platform for discarded material from exhibitions or the temporary structures being discussed in this book.

FK: Exactly. We tried to really make it professional because there are so many exhibitions and exhibition constructions, but they have to come down at the end, and you can count on this. If you go on the street or a construction site, you never know what you will find.

There is also a difference in finding materials in different cities. In Berlin it's very hard because everybody takes material from the street, but in Munich it's easier because they've been building more – there it's a paradise. Then, for example, in Zürich it's really difficult because when you go on to a construction site they're very efficient with materials. On the other hand, they are also tearing down whole areas of cities.

Let's talk about the Jellyfish Theatre at Union Street in London's Southwark, produced for the London Festival of Architecture 2010. How did that project come about?

Martin Kaltwasser: This was in collaboration with The Red Room Theatre Company, who went through the whole country looking for temporary structures and found our previously built theatre, Amphis, at Wysing Arts Centre in Cambridge. The idea was to create a temporary structure to host the Oikos Project, the first theatre festival in the UK to thematise climate change. It was also part of the London Festival of Architecture, organised by the Architecture Foundation, where visitors from all over England took part in building parts of the theatre in a two-day workshop.

The Jellyfish Theatre became the first theatre building in London completely built from scrap material. We chose the name because the jellyfish is both one of the most poisonous and the most beautiful creatures on Earth. The theatre was built by more than 100 volunteers in the shape of a jellyfish – with an organic body and tentacles. The use of found and recycled material, using hand tools, the minimal budget, and endless fun with building, joking and creating – all in the neighbourhood of one of the world's biggest financial centres – was a totally outstanding experience.

It was incredible because it was built in Southwark while the Shard was under construction. The bankers and businessmen passed by our stone-age construction site and they could feel and smell that we were the nicest, best, most enthusiastic and funniest construction site in the whole of London! The Jellyfish Theatre was mostly made out of pallets, which we got from the New Covent Garden Market as well, and old theatre sets, event sets and a lot of private material donations. It's our experience that as soon as we start a construction, we communicate a lot with passersby and visitors, and then a snowball effect starts. After a short time, everybody knows we need material and sometimes we are literally overflooded with free building material.

Did you ever return to the project after it had been completed and was being used as a theatre? Are you often involved in the events programme that accompanies your temporary structures?

MK: It's different for each project. For the Jellyfish Theatre, Red Room organised the Theatre Festival and, together with the Architecture Foundation, the application for the whole building permission. It is completely different now with the Ding Dong Dom, which is the younger sister of the Jellyfish Theatre. The Ding Dong Dom is a temporary theatre in the middle of Berlin, which we started building in summer 2013 in collaboration with the avant garde performance group Showcase

FIGURE 5.11: above / the Jellyfish Theatre was made of discarded theatre sets and hundreds of humble timber pallets sourced from New Covent Garden Market

Beat Le Mot on the site of the Holzmarkt, near Alexanderplatz. It is a work-in-progress situation: the theatre will not be completed until 2016 or thereabouts, but in May 2014 the Month of Performance Art took place in the 'unfinished' space, which had already a roof, and walls made out of more than 400 recycled windows – so it was a glass house. Many events, happenings and performances took place that summer of 2014, because everybody who came there was totally enthusiastic about the non-perfect setting, the unfinished situation, which seemingly motivates and inspires people more than a perfect situation. Therefore you can say that the perfect situation is the construction site. Maybe this is much closer to our experience in life than perfect settings.

FIGURE 5.12: above / the Jellyfish Theatre was formed organically by hand, with limited pre-prepared plans or models, and exploded outwards behind the dressing rooms to form the 'tentacles' of the jellyfish

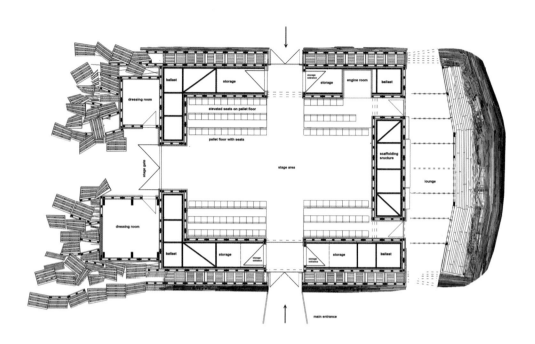

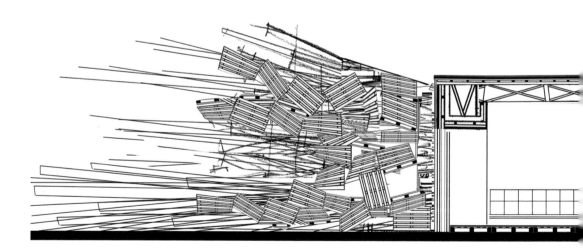

FIGURE 5.13: above top/ plan of the Jellyfish Theatre
FIGURE 5.14: above bottom / section through the Jellyfish Theatre

The Amphis in Cambridge, which you made in 2008, is still there. Would you say, then, that it is temporary or permanent?

FK: Well, this is the funny thing, it only had a permit for two years. After that two-year period it was still in really good condition – and also we have to say that it is on private land. It's a really beautiful theatre and it has an incredible acoustic quality that no one knew about when we were building it; they have a lot of musical festivals in August and the director said she loves the acoustics because it's like a dome or a church.

It took us three weeks just to do the ground work because we made it double the size than we first thought. It's really polished because we got incredible materials. We got a lot of teak wood, mainly from the colleges: half the façade is made of teak, as well as the floor and beams. People just brought us incredible materials. The thing was that an owl also made it his home, so we weren't

allowed to take the structure down. It's now under this protection somehow and nobody asks any more. Now it's permanent but it was never meant to be. Maybe we would have built it differently had we known, but the thing with temporary structures is that you can experiment more and then you think, 'Yes, this is really working, let it stand there.'

Is that perhaps why temporary structures appeal to you – because you like to experiment, and because you also build the structures yourselves, you're almost making it up as you go along?

FK: We always go with the material.

MK: Of course we make drawings, create an idea about the structure, make plans – sometimes less precise, sometimes very detailed – and then we build a basic skeleton for the theatre, the house, the shelter. This basic skeleton structure is mostly built from solid timber, mostly new,

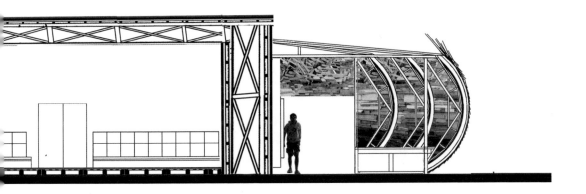

bought material, or we even use scaffolding as the basic structure (as we did for Jellyfish Theatre, Ding Dong Dom and Musterhaus). Then after having completed the basic structure we make the cladding, the building of walls, doors, and interior design from found material. In this stage of building we act very freely, very sculptural.

FK: We never create models because we don't know what the thing will look like. You can shape it a little, but you never know how a façade will look until you're there. The Jellyfish Theatre was supposed to look totally different; some things didn't work or they weren't allowed, or you suddenly find a different material. For the Amphis Theatre in Cambridge it was also like this: we had volunteers and they created the façade. You never know how it's going to turn out until the end.

Is the appearance of your temporary structures important to you?

FK: Somehow it's always a struggle because of course it's important what it looks like, especially from inside, but sometimes you have to make compromises, or sometimes it's really hard and you have to rework elements.

Do you see these temporary structures as art, installation or architecture, or something in between?

FK: I am an artist. My role was really to look for a site or for materials. Maybe you don't have to see it as art or architecture; maybe it's an effort to create something that you would like to have in a city, maybe you don't need this big planning permission. In Germany we have this word

FIGURE 5.15: above / the structure of the Amphis Theatre was built on a falsework of pallets and timber beams, filled with compressed sand and rubble because concrete was too expensive

FIGURE 5.16: above top / Amphis Theatre is an octagonal two-storey theatre on the site of Wysing Arts Centre in Cambridgeshire made of discarded materials, built in 2008
FIGURE 5.17: above bottom / part of the façade of Amphis Theatre is made up of old salvaged doors and windows

'Möglichkeitssinn' that means the sense of possibilities or opportunities – that something is possible but you would never have thought it. For example, with the Jellyfish Theatre, it was just, 'Wow, here is a structure for £5,000, standing right in front of the Renzo Piano building which costs billions.'

Are there any constraints or challenges to a temporary project?

FK: The more regulations we have, the more you have to calculate everything and in the end it becomes impossible to work with recycled material. As soon as a project gets a special status and becomes more public, we cannot take responsibility any more, or an institution can't take responsibility, and as soon as it goes to the municipality, it's really difficult because then who takes responsibility?

In fact, I don't want to do this any more and Martin is going more and more in this direction, because for me, the freedom of creating is missing and then you are totally into architecture. You cannot work with the material any more. If you don't like something, you cannot just exchange it. If you have a planned building, everything is clear, but as soon as you work with the material it's a totally different process. A lot of people don't like it because it's so situationalist, a little bit chaotic and much more time consuming. On the other hand, what we've always said is that you're getting structures you never expect, because all of a sudden the structures form. Sometimes it's just down to coincidence. If you have a totally planned process you'll never have those coincidences.

FIGURE 5.18: above /discarded material picked up from the streets of Zürich was used to create this site-specific 'palais' in 2007

FIGURE 5.19: above / with its wide, overhanging roof, the structure became a popular meeting place in this Zürich square

INTERVIEW 11 /
PLASTIQUE FANTASTIQUE

MARCO
CANEVACCI

Plastique Fantastique is a Berlin-based platform for temporary architecture, founded by Marco Canevacci, which samples the performative possibilities of urban environments. Established in 1999, Plastique Fantastique has been influenced by the unique circumstances that made the city a laboratory for temporary spaces and has specialised in creating pneumatic installations as alternative, adaptable, low-energy spaces for temporary and ephemeral activities. The transparent, lightweight and mobile shell structures relate to the notion of activating, creating and sharing public space and involving citizens in creative processes. At the moment Plastique Fantastique develops project-oriented teams to realise a wide range of projects worldwide, from London's Clerkenwell Design Week to a recent teaching workshop in Cyprus.

How did you start Plastique Fantastique?

Marco Canevacci: The real beginning was in the early 1990s. I moved to Berlin in 1991 and I was studying architecture at the technical university. At the same time I was quite impressed with the underground life there: you had this special sensitivity about temporary spaces since the East German state collapsed, so everybody was proposing a mix of cultural and hedonistic activities in all the abandoned areas you might find in the middle of East Berlin, which were quite a lot. I had come from Rome, which was quite the opposite situation.

At the end of the 1990s I finished my studies and rented an empty factory of 2,000 sq m in the area of Friedrichshain. Since it was impossible to heat it, I, together with some friends (Michael Heim, Pietro Balp, Raffaele Distefano), started to make some bubbles and fill them with hot air. That was the beginning of the experience. Nowadays I work very closely with a musician (Marco Barotti), a sculptor (Markus Wüste) and a designer (Yena Young).

What drove you to work with plastic and these inflated forms?

MC: Actually, it was this situation: the necessity of having a warm place inside this big factory. Plastic – I'm talking about polyethylene – is quite a cheap material; you can easily seal it and create these kind of basic bubbles. We filled it with warm air and that was it. They were the first rooms that we produced, in 1999. That was the beginning, and afterwards I realised the potential of designing these kind of architectures and we started to move around Europe doing different installations.

So the name Plastique Fantastique came out of what you were creating?

MC: The name itself was actually the name of the first installation we did in our empty factory, which in the end transformed itself into a techno club called Deli an der Schillingbrücke. Since then we have kept the name.

What interests you about temporary architecture? Are all your projects temporary?

MC: I think there's something magical about a structure popping up in 20 minutes and at the same time disappearing as fast as it inflates itself, so you can create an extra architecture in a public space that exists for a limited span of time. I'm interested in this because with standard architecture it takes a really long time to express yourself and after a couple of years you might have something different in your mind.

How do you hope people react to these structures? What do you hope their experience will be?

MC: Most of our installations are quite playful works, so people actually get quite relaxed and start to play within the one they are in as well as outside the bubble. So it creates a communicative environment at once. It's a public thing, because people who don't know each other start to interact, communicate and interchange the experience you may have in this context. Of course you can add different layers, performances, audio systems, projections and so on to enhance a project itself.

FIGURE 5.20: previous / the shape of Aeropolis was able to adapt around existing structures and squash itself in between trees and lamp posts

FIGURE 5.21: above / a gold ring wrapped itself around a building for the Kunst- und Kultur Festival in Berlin in 2011

Let's talk about the The Emotion Maker at Clerkenwell Design Week in 2011. How did that project come about and what was the idea behind it?

MC: The project was first of all a collaboration between three people: myself, a sound experience designer called Lorenzo Brusci and a musician, Marco Barotti. We wanted to offer a concert which was always changing, so you enter the structure and you can choose from 15 different instruments playing hundreds of music samples pre-recorded by different musicians to create a composition of your own. Only two people were allowed to enter the installation at one time, it took 10 minutes, and the experience inside was always a different one. It's funny because in most cases the two people didn't know each other: you have to put your name on a list and then you

go inside with the other person. Sometimes we had wonderful concerts, sometimes it was weird, anyhow it was always different.

How much are you involved with the events programmes that go along with your structures? Is that an important side of the project, what goes on during the time the structure is up?

MC: The structure is actually a tool to play with the urban landscape, so you use the bubble as a tool and then you have to add something on to it. It can be something like an installation, but it can also be a banquet – you could just invite the neighbours to cook something inside and share food together. We did this project in 2014 called Sound of Light and in this case we offered a synesthetic approach to experiencing light as

FIGURE 5.22: above / the Emotion Maker housed an all-consuming, interactive sound installation that could be experienced by only two people at a time

sound, so basically there is this opaque pneumatic architecture, and once you are inside you have light coming through six different hanging columns, each representing a basic colour: cyan, magenta and yellow, and red, green and blue.

There is a camera mounted on the rooftop of the structure – a music pavilion in Hamm, Germany, that we squeezed the installation into – which films the sky and divides it into the six colours. The output is transformed into sound and converted from visible to audible sensory input. At the bottom of each column, a woofer reacts directly to the sound and the lighting conditions, converting the whole architecture into a giant vibrating loudspeaker.

What happens to your projects afterwards? Do they get reused?

MC: It depends. We have been trying to re-present Sound of Light in different locations, but we have to change it in order for it to fit in other places. It was a fun idea to place it inside a former music pavilion in Germany, a building of 1912, and now we are proposing it in a different context. For example, one is in France, where they also have different music pavilions. We would like to include all of it inside a major structure, so the pneumatic structure sits around the music pavilion, you have to enter it and it becomes a new vibrating architecture – something unusual and something new.

There are projects that we've done that have been reinterpreted for other conditions, and

FIGURE 5.23: above / the Emotion Maker broke down the boundaries between strangers and the public space within a city

FIGURE 5.24: above top / Sound of Light placed an inflatable structure into an early 20th-century music pavilion in Hamm, Germany in 2014

FIGURE 5.25: above bottom /Plastique Fantastique used a digital camera to transform sunlight from the sky above to audible frequencies with a series of woofers

there are basic geometrical forms that you can use several times. During the Metropolis Festival 2013 in Copenhagen, we had an installation called Aeropolis. The pneumatic structure was designed with two optional tops (one mirrored and one transparent) to allow maximum mobility and flexibility during its tour through 13 different locations around the city. It offered a communication platform for experiencing a sequence of activities with changing scenographies, all curated together with local cultural institutions: astronomy between two climbing walls in Nørrebro, kindergarten and hip-hop in front of a supermarket in Valby, meditation and yoga by a lake in Vanløse, performances at Islands Brygge, martial arts at Superkilen, lectures in Amager, a silent disco at one of the noisiest intersections of the city in Nordvest... If you take it as it is, it's just a geometric shape, but if you try to squeeze it into the existing environment it starts to change its shape and become something different, something you can apply to endless situations. So I'm more interested in squeezing or pressing or playing with the local context than in placing a bubble in the middle of a square.

Do you mean inside a building, rather than in a public space like a street or a square?

MC: I'd rather try to play with the neighbourhood, with the existing buildings or trees or bridges, than place it on a square. I always try to change the shape and the environment itself by having a contact. You can place a bubble in a narrow street and it changes its shape and the street changes character as well – and you can do that in a couple of minutes, half an hour maximum.

FIGURE 5.26: right / the transparent bubble of Aeropolis popped up around different locations in Copenhagen in 2013

That probably also changes a person's perception or experience of that street or space.

MC: You can wake up, go out and your street has changed, you don't have the street itself, you have something in between that is offering an experience or some weird shapes.

Do you notice a difference depending on where or in which country you place these structures? Do people react differently in different cities?

MC: Yes, of course. You may have different reactions if you work in the south of Europe or in Scandinavia, but I always realise that there is some basic stuff that doesn't change. People are always interested in it, they come and ask, and once you've asked them to come and experience the installation, they do it. The feedback we get is mostly good and it's something that's always quite interesting. Every time we do these projects there is no aggression wherever we work – in Berlin, in Spain. We also always invite people to help us during the set-up, the dismantling and the installation itself, so it's quite important to be on site, to invite people to check out our work and to deal with it.

FIGURE 5.27: above top / a boxing match takes place outside one of the Aeropolis's locations in Copenhagen
FIGURE 5.28: above bottom / Aeropolis was made of fireproof PVC, with industrial ventilators to keep the shape blown up
FIGURE 5.29: opposite / a pneumatic sound installation, titled Space Invaders, is installed between two buildings in the Mitte district of Berlin in 2008

Nowadays we are making lots of workshops, mostly with students, and of course with people that are just passing by. Maybe they get interested and we make a quick introduction about how to use this kind of architecture – the easiest way is to get plastic film taped altogether, then you just need a normal ventilator and that's it, so I think it's quite good to offer the basic knowhow to let people create these structures by themselves.

Do you think temporary architecture is becoming more popular with students? What advice would you give to a student wishing to go in a similar direction?

MC: At the moment there is a big revival of all those kind of utopian approaches of the 1960s. I think that most of the architecture or design universities are trying to reapproach this way of working with temporary architecture and inflatable architecture is one-fifth of that, so it's quite popular. I had a workshop in Cyprus last November, and next week I'm going back to produce, with students, three different structures that will be going around the island of Cyprus over two and a half weeks. We also had an open call with local artists to play with those bubbles.

What else does the future hold for Plastique Fantastique?

MC: There are three main directions. One is all the experiences I am making with students within universities – workshops and the like. The second one is the more artistic projects, for example getting invited to a festival and having the freedom to develop anything you want. And thirdly, there are the more commercial projects, where you just make a commitment to build an installation for an event, fair or presentation. Then there are the collaborations, with different artists and professionals.

What would be your dream project?

MC: To make a science fiction movie with Quentin Tarantino! That's a good brief isn't it? I love his movies, because they're quite ironic and this is my approach. There are lots of directors I would like to work with but I think I would like to work on fiction. When you work with a camera you can choose what to film and what not to film. When there is a performance on a stage or in one of our structures, the public can see everything, but with a camera you choose what people look at.

CHAPTER 06 /
THE ART WORLD AND TEMPORARY ARCHITECTURE: THE MEETING OF TWO DISCIPLINES

INTERVIEWS:
GRUPPE [Switzerland] / Morag Myerscough [UK]

By its very nature, temporary architecture can be hard to pin down to a specific discipline. It can be architecture, public realm and urban design but it can also be art, installation or exhibition. The definition of roles can be further diluted, often for the better, by collaborations between architects, artists, photographers and writers. Developers and arts groups are opening their eyes to the value of a more fluid design process that involves multiple actors from different creative disciplines collaborating and learning from each other. This chapter gives examples of designers inspired by work outside their field, architects working with artists, and initiatives combining the two.

THIS IS TEMPORARY

One example is Zürich-based practice GRUPPE, which is concerned with thinking through building and the political nature of architecture, often inviting like-minded creatives, architects, thinkers and designers to participate in talks and debates. GRUPPE explains here how, following a project at Art Basel, it met British artist Richard Wentworth, who then invited the practice to collaborate on a project at Stanton Williams-designed Central Saint Martins in London.

The resulting work, Black Maria, was a pop-up wooden auditorium that sat in the atrium of the art and design school for four weeks in 2013. Inspired by Thomas Edison's first film production studio of the same name, the structure was designed as an informal meeting point and place of exchange, based around discussions, performance and film. Says GRUPPE co-founder Nicholas Lobo Brennan: 'A lot of what we do is about getting in touch with people and trying to have genuine discussions about things that we feel are important.' Built entirely from the cheapest wood, it comprised an 'inhabitable billboard' inspired by building site hoardings, with a stepped auditorium behind it for presentations and talks. A large hole in the billboard façade allowed events to spill onto the college's main thoroughfare and let passersby peer into the space. 'We tried to design it so that some things were suggested,' Brennan explains, 'but as much as possible, we tried to make it unexpected. Contemporary architecture is extremely codified.' In a very restrictive space, lined with security gates to stop the general public entering the school, this project transformed a neutral crossroads into a place for people and students to meet, gather, eat lunch and chat. A precedent for Black Maria can also be

FIGURE 6.1: previous / Temple of Agape, a collaboration between Morag Myerscough and Luke Morgan, was a temporary pavilion created for the Festival of Love on London's South Bank in 2014

FIGURE 6.2: above / the 'inhabitable billboard' of Black Maria by GRUPPE was inspired by building site hoardings in King's Cross, London found in Wentworth's project An Area of Outstanding Unnatural Beauty, created for Artangel in 2002, which encouraged visitors to see apparently unremarkable shops and alleyways around King's Cross in a new light.

Although GRUPPE is quick to say it 'does architecture' – 'we don't do art projects, we don't do performance' – projects like the Black Maria and House of Muses, an inhabitable white plaster column installed outside the Museum of London, share a commonality with the rule-breaking art world. Lobo Brennan explains in the interview how and why so many of GRUPPE's projects are self-initiated, suggesting that one reason is that competitions have become risk-averse and less open to new ideas: 'We were very interested, from the beginning, in a way of working that meant doing things straight away, as directly as possible, rather than doing competitions, which means doing miniaturised structures for bigger things that come later. What we were trying to do was build up a series of ideas about architecture.' GRUPPE's projects attempt to open up possibilities, discover other paths and deal with notions of ambiguity and incompleteness in spaces that are often institutional or authoritarian. They see architecture as a way of thinking and acting, where the gathering of materials into a structure is inseparable from the assembly of people for the events, debates, and participation during its lifetime. Whether installation, art or architecture, the aim is to give new perspective on a particular urban space. 'For me, in the end, the most important thing is what is embedded in the actual architecture, what the actual thing itself does,' says Lobo Brennan.

FIGURE 6.3: above / a talk takes place in Black Maria, with audiences either side of the threshold

THIS IS TEMPORARY

Black Maria itself was part of RELAY, a nine-year arts programme set up to enliven the new public spaces cropping up around the King's Cross development site and turn the area into a destination for discovering international contemporary art. Drawing on King's Cross's heritage as a transport interchange and its future as an emerging cityscape, the first three year period has been curated by Michael Pinsky and Stéphanie Delcroix and includes King's Cross Pond Club (2015). This was a temporary natural bathing pool, designed by Dutch architects Ooze (Eva Pfannes and Sylvain Hartenberg) and the Ljubljana- and Berlin-based artist Marjetica Potrc, that aimed to make visitors to King's Cross think about the relationship between nature and the urban environment. Surrounded by busy building sites, the 40m-long pond was purified and filtered through a closed-loop process using wetland and submerged water plants as a commentary on consumption and the changing nature of undeveloped spaces. Ooze and Potrc would collaborate again in 2014, creating a Wind Lift – a wind powered lift that carried people to the top of the Ford Road Viaduct – for the Folkestone Triennial.

At the opposite end of the spectrum, London-based artist and designer Morag Myerscough uses her background in graphics and inspiration from the architecture world to create pop-up exhibitions, installations, wayfinding projects and pavilions festooned with strong flashes of colour, pattern and type. Operating under the banner Studio Myerscough, she's a one-woman band with an instantly recognisable style, but Myerscough also frequently collaborates with former *Architects' Journal* editor Isabel Allen, curator Claire Catterall and artist Luke Morgan, together known as Supergroup. Myerscough's projects are characterised by a bold, playful aesthetic that engages audiences and builds an identity for an area. She explains that her interest in temporary architecture was sparked by The Deptford Project, an abandoned commuter train that was transformed into a café in 2008. Part of a wider project to regenerate the disused railway yard of Deptford Station, the carriage looked onto Deptford High Street and was decorated with images inspired by local history. The interior was kitted out with bespoke, hand-painted stools and an 'Elvis Presley' loo by Morgan was set up in a garden shed on the adjoining terrace. 'I really wanted to make it a space for the local community, a place that was uplifting with a platform to sit out on in good weather,' she says. 'The train was meant to be there for 18 months but lasted five years and became embedded in the community.'

Since then, she's collaborated with architect Allford Hall Monaghan Morris (AHMM) on various projects and forged an ongoing relationship with developer Cathedral Group. She has designed exhibits for London's Design Museum and created the exterior of the Peter Cook-curated British Pavilion for the 2004 Venice Biennale of Architecture (at the time he said she had given the building 'a new frock and some bright jewellery'). 'Now what I do is a lot of things that are about belonging,' she reflects. 'I have to provide enough flexibility in those spaces for people to enable them to make it their own. Now I try to involve people in the design process. It's very much about getting people excited.'

Another of her projects, The Movement Café, was a temporary café and performance space next to Greenwich's DLR station in south-east London. Built from scratch in just 16 days to coincide with the opening of the 2012 Olympics, it sat on the site of the former Greenwich Industrial Estate currently being regenerated by Cathedral (the developers didn't want the gateway to the Olympic borough to be an unattractive construction site). The eye-catching shipping container structure, built in the centre of an amphitheatre-like space, was adorned with large, vibrant, hand-painted wooden panels spelling out tweets by Olympic Poet Lemn Sissay, such as 'This is the House' and 'This is the Path'. Myerscough and Luke Morgan made furniture from reclaimed laboratory tops, while cushions were handsewn from kite fabric. As well as a café, the space played host to storytelling, poetry reading and acoustic performances. The idea was 'to get people thinking about this area being a destination place and not just to walk on by – to connect with the local community which had just walked past this site for many years,' explains Myerscough.

A year later, The Pavilion, a collaboration with Luke Morgan, was a temporary pavilion installed in the lobby of Mecanoo's new Library of Birmingham. Designed to house an 18-week programme of creative residencies, the single-storey timber construction hosted artists, filmmakers and a range of other creatives. Myerscough describes it as a 'curiosity box', closed at night but opening up to become a new space each week depending on what each resident had planned. Like the Movement Café, it was topped with bright neon signs featuring words inspired by workshops held with young arts group Birmingham 2022. 'We wanted to greet visitors with a smile and a celebration of the word,' she says. 'It encourages conversation and fun.' Built in just two weeks, the outer walls were hand-painted with symbols used in online communication, such as questions marks and ampersands, while the inside was kept simple and flexible for the different art groups, with battens used as ad hoc shelves.

FIGURE 6.4: above / the Movement Café by Morag Myerscough was a temporary café and performance space next to Greenwich's DLR station in south east London in 2012

FIGURE 6.5: above / the Pavilion, a collaboration between Morag Myerscough and Luke Morgan in 2013, was a temporary
pavilion installed in the lobby of Mecanoo's new Library of Birmingham

Myerscough says she hates labels and limitations, and in the interview explains that she would prefer her work to be defined neither as art nor architecture. She sees these labels as a result of the prescribed route of design education, where students have to pick one thing or another and then stick to it. She suggests that the boundaries between disciplines could be more blurred. For her, the design process is the most important thing, no matter how one defines temporary architecture: 'I have not tried to do art or architecture. I'm just making work,' she says of her projects – whether it be painting hundreds of boards into the middle of the night, for example, or getting local people involved with the creation of the project as much as possible. For her, it is about creating a sense of belonging – places that people can connect to and be part of.

This chapter hopes to show that collaborations between artists and architects, and designers taking on the role of architect in these types of projects, can foster a sense of creative possibility and the recognition that there are multiple ways of doing things. Yet perhaps, as Myerscough says, the result doesn't need to be defined as art or architecture; maybe a new word is needed to describe this temporal process. As Folke Köbberling, also an artist, notes in the previous chapter on Materiality: 'In Germany we have this word "Möglichkeitssinn" that means the sense of possibilities or opportunities – that something is possible but you would never have thought it.'

INTERVIEW 12 /
GRUPPE

INTERVIEW WITH:
NICHOLAS LOBO BRENNAN

GRUPPE is an architecture and design practice established by Christoph Junk, Boris Gusic and Nicholas Lobo Brennan in Zürich in 2010. Its work is concerned with thinking through building and the inherently political nature of architecture. It sees architecture as a way of thinking and acting, where the gathering of materials is inseparable from the assembly of people. Junk, Gusic and Lobo Brennan teach together at ETH Zürich and have been visiting critics at architecture schools in Switzerland, UK and the Netherlands. GRUPPE won the 2012 Swiss Art Award for Architecture, exhibited during Art Basel 2012, and was shortlisted for the Lisbon 2013 Triennale Debut Award.

How did you establish GRUPPE?

Nicholas Lobo Brennan: Christoph Junk, Boris Gusic and I started working together in 2011. We decided to formalise what we were doing by giving ourselves a name; we didn't want to use our surnames and all of us liked very much the many Gruppes, grupos or groups of the past, the Independent Group being a British example. We were very interested in these first, second and third wave Modernist groups, who were somehow linking up quite similar aesthetic concerns involving social and political issues. The use of the word group is somehow inherent in that. Everyone involved in GRUPPE is an architect or does architectural projects. In that sense – we don't do art projects, we don't do performance – what we do is architecture.

What percentage of your projects would you say are temporary? How has temporary architecture shaped your practice?

NLB: We were very interested, from the beginning, in a way of working that meant doing things straight away, as directly as possible, rather than doing competitions, which means doing miniaturised structures for bigger things that come later. That meant that the projects at the beginning were self-initiated and temporary, but what we were trying to do was build up a series of ideas about architecture, and you could say those are kind of permanent. Some of those ideas that were being developed are now being put into permanent projects such as housing. We don't see it like 'Here's some temporary stuff and that's completely different from the permanent stuff.' For us, it's one continuous stream, where you develop ideas in one field and it transfers to another and vice versa.

What was the reason behind starting your practice with self-initiated projects and not competitions?

NLB: The reason not to do competitions is because if you look back at the early part and middle of the 20th century, competitions were really forms for new ideas, whereas today for, shall we say permanent architecture, they have become a way to avoid risk. Competitions used to be an opportunity to open up new possibilities.

I would say that there has been a culture change, and in many cases the purpose of a competition has inverted. What that means is that if you are just doing competitions, you're trying to devise solutions, but those solutions might not even be for the right questions. The purpose of development today is primarily financial, to do with capital, and that's becoming increasingly the ultimate end. Anything which is social is an add-on. I guess we're trying to find ways around it and discover other paths.

Do you think temporary architecture offers more possibilities than permanent architecture? Does it allow architects to be more experimental, more creative perhaps?

NLB: I think temporary architecture has for a long, long time been a form of experimentation. If the competitions aren't experimental any more, then temporary architecture still is. It's not blanket true that competitions don't allow for experimentation but definitely, if you go back to the 1950s and 1960s, it was incredible all the things you could do. Today temporary architecture certainly does still allow you to experiment – and I don't mean mindlessly experiment, I mean seriously propose more relevant ways of building for people today.

What is your starting point for self-initiated projects? Do you involve any other participants – artists, designers, the public or the local community?

NLB: I would say the absolute first, most important thing, is the commitment to doing it. Then you have to wonder what is the basis for that commitment. For me personally it was about the fact that we're building a world in a very particular way, with these pretty poor concessions to a bit of the social added on to large developments. So I was very interested in the relationship between the form and material of architecture and its social functions. One way I like to describe architecture is that the assembly of materials is inseparable from the gathering of people. What are the implications of that? It's to do with who builds it and who uses it, and it's

deeply political in that sense. I was thinking about how we could make a world in a way that was renewed politically, and more socially minded or democratic. There didn't seem to be any particular vehicles to do that. The thinking was, 'OK, let's just try and build places that have some of these properties that we're thinking about.'

Then it became a case of this idea of reuse, which is a bit overkilled now unfortunately. We started to collect materials – disused plywood from particularly over-the-top architecture exhibitions, for instance – and to think about how we could use it. At the same time, it was a case of just going out and meeting people, while contributing to discussions, debates, and essentially talking to people about what architecture could be. We started to do these self-initiated projects and eventually we began to be invited to do

FIGURE 6.6: previous / Black Maria was a collaboration between GRUPPE and Richard Wentworth at Central Saint Martins in London's King Cross

FIGURE 6.7: above / Black Maria was designed as an informal meeting point and place of exchange

different things. We did a series of small projects in cultural spaces: for instance, we made a small auditorium standing on legs that was designed to be disassembled and put in the back of our van to be carried around to different points in Switzerland. We were at Art Basel and met the artist Richard Wentworth. We're interested not just in the structure but in the events that go along with the structure, so we invited him to come and give a talk. A lot of what we do is about getting in touch with people and trying to have genuine discussions about things that we feel are important.

Let's talk about Black Maria, a pop-up wooden auditorium you created with Richard Wentworth in the atrium of Central Saint Martins for the arts organisation RELAY in 2013. How did that project came about and what it was like working with an artist?

NLB: He invited us off the back of our project at Art Basel. One of the main ideas of our project was the concept of a narthex – the entrance of a church, where elements of the profane can come in, so you'd have markets there, even prostitutes and the homeless. Churches are the ultimate institution, where the authorities embody the very material of the architecture, so to have a space

that was allowing non-institutional things to occur, from a modern point of view, was very intriguing.

Did that lead you to Central Saint Martins?

NLB: Richard suggested that Central Saint Martins had a potential narthex – this huge hall. He said, 'I'd like you to come over and develop something along the lines of what you did in Basel.' And it is a kind of narthex, really, because you go in and there's no point to the space; it's basically a big lobby. It's like the biggest corridor in London, basically. What was intriguing was that you go into this big corridor space and then you come up against a security barrier. At the old school you could just go in and out, a much better condition for a school like Saint Martins to be in. Now it has this sort of education castle with this huge hall in front – it's a gated community, a very restrictive space. So we found that it was the ultimate expression of all the stuff we were trying not to do, and we just said, 'OK, let's do it!' It was seeing the potential in what Stanton Williams had proposed, but also seeing the weaknesses.

Why is it called Black Maria? What is the concept around it?

NLB: The first thing was to think how we could make something that sat right next to this big hall but was really a place for showing and making work. The Black Maria was the name of Thomas Edison's cinema-making machine, which was one of the first film studios, if not the first. The original Black Maria was normal, everyday architecture, with a pitched roof, but strange things could happen: the roofs could open to allow light in,

FIGURE 6.8: left / behind the flat 'inhabitable billboard' was a stepped auditorium for presentations, film screenings and talks

or the whole thing could rotate to control lighting conditions. What we had was something similar: a normal, everyday construction, set up in such a way that lots of different possibilities could happen. We tried to design it so that some of those things were suggested, but as much as possible we tried to make it unexpected. Contemporary architecture is extremely codified.

It took us three weeks to build – a very big structure for a very small team. The whole thing was made from the cheapest wood around. The idea was not just to take it and accept those materials for what they do, but to provide new ways of looking at everything: the materials themselves, their use and their function. You could build it anywhere, it's not made out of some special material; it's just the material you can get wherever.

How involved were you with the events programme?

NLB: There were several events run by King's Cross, then Richard had his own series and there were open events for the public and anyone from the school. We ended up having quite a full, dense, varied programme. The structure was double-sided, so you ended up having this nice interaction between the inside and the outside. People walking past could see the cinema screen or you could have the audience on the inside and the outside. People started to use the space quite informally or meet there. Putting up a new façade meant it wasn't a corridor any more – it became a square. It was a small architectural move but it made quite a difference. We really viewed this as a place in the city, it became a small piece of city.

FIGURE 6.9: above / the stepped auditorium could be used as a stage, with the audience peering in through the façade's opening

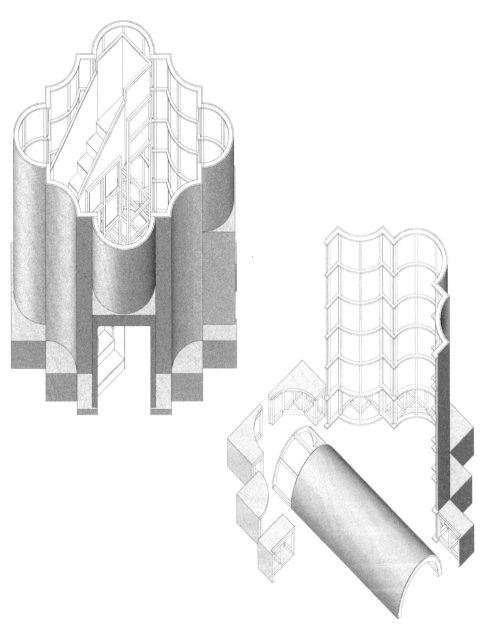

FIGURE 6.10: above left / Axionometric drawing of House of Muses
FIGURE 6.11: above right / the structure was made of panels that were supported by wooden batons

What happened to Black Maria afterwards? Did it have an afterlife?

NLB: This is something I'm not sure exactly about and something that I'm quite disappointed with – the status of the project is a bit unknown. We agreed originally that we would take it apart and then reassemble it around October or November 2015. They occasionally make noises but we'd be very upset if the materials go to waste because all of them are reusable. A lot of architects have this sort of materiality fetish, where things become entirely pointless – 'Let's use a really special wood, or let's cut it in a way where you cannot possibly reuse it again' – but I thought it was important for the project to have another life afterwards. Let's see.

Let's talk about the House of Muses at the Museum of London in 2014. How did that project come about?

NLB: It was a competition and someone told us to send something in. We didn't even know about it at first. We got into the next round which was quite interesting because so had Sam Jacob of FAT and Pablo Bronstein, two heroes of mine. Then it was like, 'OK, this is quite serious, let's go for it.' It suddenly seemed like it was a serious discussion then. It wasn't like it was just a competition to make something pretty.

What was the concept for the House of Muses?

NLB: From the beginning we were interested in the fact that the site is in the Barbican. It's surrounded by the city, with these megastructures from today – huge, often glass buildings, kind of mountains, almost – and then you get these slightly more utopian megastructures of the 1960s

and 1970s. It almost has a surreal scale. The site there is perhaps one of the most intense moments in London. At the same time, when you walk around the area, there are these weird little fragments – a little bit of Roman Britain, a bit of Tudor Britain, and there's a little fragment of a Sir Christopher Wren church standing on a traffic island. The Museum of London is wondering what it should do about its future. The building is quite problematic because it's very restrictive – the entrance is almost impossible to find.

We wanted to add our own historic fragment, so we imagined that there was once a megastructure at the scale of St Paul's and that all we're left with now is one fragment at one end and one fragment at the other end. House of Muses is slightly gothic in character but it's formed of elements of classical architecture. Pre-modern architecture has a sort of institutional authority to it, which we thought was quite interesting to put in front of a museum which was wondering if it was institutional or authoritarian enough.

We created a semi-monumental object with a staircase inside it and benches on the edges – so you get the language and scale of a monument, but that monumentality is broken or subverted by the fact that people can just sit on it or pop up their head out the top. It was exactly like a stage set: there was this very finished, clean exterior, but inside, it's the breaking of the illusion where you can see behind the scenes.

What did you hope people took away from the House of Muses?

NLB: You had this typical corporate architecture at the entrance to the Museum, white and dull, not allowing for chance encounters and places to meet. You couldn't have picked a worse site,

FIGURE 6.12: above / a wooden staircase inside House of Muses takes visitors up to peep over the top of the structure

under the canopy of the Museum of London, but it had great potential because, a bit like at Central Saint Martins, it is a moment when people are passing through. One of the things we noticed with the House of Muses is that you started to get all these unsolicited events that, I would say, characterise city life. For example, a woman in her fifties used to keep coming back and would just sit there and read for hours.

We tried to imbue the House of Muses with all the qualities of what a city should be. That's why temporary architecture is quite important, because maybe it becomes a laboratory for what the future of the city should be. I hope there could be a chance to use some of these ideas to really contribute to making what a city should be.

Are you concerned with what similar practices are doing with temporary structures?

NLB: I really like We Made That, Raumlabor and Assemble a lot and I think what they do is fantastic. We don't look at them to find out what they're doing, but I think we share certain concerns and I think there should be more architecture like it. I'm interested in a book like this because it brings people together.
One thing I would like to say is that there are different ways to do things. You might deal only with the state, or with private clients, or with actively social causes, and I think there is a slight hierarchy regarding what is more 'correct'.

But for me, in the end, the most important thing is what is embedded in the actual architecture, what

FIGURE 6.13: above / the panels of House of Muses being assembled outside Museum of London

FIGURE 6.14: above / House of Muses was conceived as a large stone architectural fragment outside the Museum of London in 2014

the actual thing itself does. The political nature of it is contained within the details – by 'political' I don't mean supporting the right party or the right causes, but that architecture is often organised in such a way that it closes down possibilities. How can you open up possibilities? That's to do with working with ambiguity and incompleteness, two very difficult things to work with.

The projects described here, though temporary, are somehow working with the problems of the permanent. All the things we are talking about can be realised in a permanent project, but at the same time we are trying to bring energy, lightness and the event. That's why I find it difficult to distinguish between the temporary and the permanent – the issues each tries to solve are somehow the same.

FIGURE 6.15: above / House of Muses was like a stage set, with a polished, pristine exterior and a scaffolding interior

INTERVIEW 13 /
MORAG MYERSCOUGH

MORAG
MYERSCOUGH

Morag Myerscough is a London-based designer who founded her multidisciplinary company Studio Myerscough in 1993 and founded Supergroup with Luke Morgan in 2010. Characterised by its engaging boldness, Myerscough's work creates specific, local responses to each distinct audience that will see and experience the design, building community and identity. She makes places from spaces that people like to be in, that stimulate and often make you smile. Ultimately, Myerscough creates and curates many different types of work, from the conversion of a train to a café, installations, numerous exhibitions and even a temple of love.

How did you start Studio Myerscough and get into creating temporary structures and pavilions?

Morag Myerscough: It goes right back to when I was at the Royal College of Art. I was making opera sets instead of posters, but everybody was worried that I would leave and be unemployable. It seemed like a guilty pleasure, so I thought I'd better buckle down and do real work and set up Studio Myerscough for my graphic work. But over time I needed to diversify and started working on lots of different exhibition designs. Then in 2002, I was very bored and needed a new outlet. I met Luke Morgan (the founder member of Supergrouplondon), who was a musician and artist and who made me realise that I had to get back to what I was originally doing. We set up Her House, where I transformed my kitchen in my house into a gallery, and we just started making things we wanted. We put our work on show at Designer's Block and I have not looked back since.

How did the Deptford Project come about?

MM: I had worked for years with the property developer Cathedral Group and they had a derelict railway yard where the building works had been put on hold due to the financial crisis – this was in 2007 – so they wanted to do something with the yard as it was in view of everybody in the middle of the high street. They thought, 'Why not a train?' and they approached me and said, 'Morag, we want to get a train and make it into a café – will you do it for us? We have a great local creative person called Rebecca Molina who would run it, we just need you to convert it.' It was an amazing project. How often are you given a full size train to play

with? I really wanted to make it a space for the local community, a place that was uplifting with a platform to sit out on in good weather surrounded by plants. I bought all the plants from Columbia Road and planted them. From the minute I went to choose our train at Shoeburyness I knew I wanted to take all the seats out and make it an open space, painted white. If I was given another train now, I would probably do it differently, but it felt right for this place. The train was meant to be there for 18 months but lasted five years and became embedded in the community. Projects like this need dedicated people to make them work; Rebecca put her whole soul into the project and it was a sad day when it had to be removed. Places need people and life to activate them, and I don't mind, once I have handed over the work, that they are added to or changed and the people using it make it their own, as we do in our homes.

What was the concept behind the Movement Café in London (2012), and how did the collaborations with Lemn Sissay come about?

MM: The Movement Café was again something we did with the Cathedral Group. The location was a building site being prepared for a huge building scheme, but the 2012 Olympics were going to start and it was just next to the Greenwich DLR station, and the council was not happy that the first thing people saw when getting off the train was a building site. So they really wanted Cathedral to do something quickly. Cathedral had been thinking about building a temporary café to get people thinking about this area being a destination place and not just to walk on by – to connect with the local community which had just walked past this site for many years. So they got me to the site and said, 'Here

FIGURE 6.16: previous / the Movement Café hosted storytelling, poetry reading and acoustic performances and featured furniture made from reclaimed laboratory tops

you are, Morag – we need a cafe ASAP!' I went home that evening completely shellshocked, thinking, 'What am I going to do?' Fortunately I had been speaking with Lemn Sissay about a larger permanent public art commission for the site and we had been talking about tweets and how the limitations on the word count were interesting. That night I just thought, 'I will look at Lemn's tweets to see if I can get any inspiration,' and the first one I read was:

'THIS IS THE HOUSE. THIS IS THE PATH. THIS IS THE GATE. THIS IS THE OPENING. THIS IS THE MORNING. THIS IS A PERSON PASSING. THIS IS EYE CONTACT.'

That was it, I knew it was right, and I just went straight into making a physical scale model. I finished it late into the night and was pleased but thought I had

better sleep on it. In the morning I was still happy so I sent it to Cathedral and they immediately said, 'Yes – make it!' We had three weeks to build it ready for the first day of the Olympics. Making is so important to me. I don't just want to hand things over to a contractor. We make as many elements as possible ourselves. I have no fear of painting hundreds of boards if I have to with a tight deadline. The process is so important to me – starting with a sketch and taking it right to the very end with as much involvement as possible. Also getting people to help us make things is important, so people have a sense of ownership. Then people gain love and care for the project they're part of. And painting is a great way of people getting involved without needing pre-learned skills.

FIGURE 6.17: above / the Deptford Project, a collaboration between Morag Myerscough and Luke Morgan, turned an abandoned commuter train into a cafe in 2008

What happens to your structures afterwards? Do you reuse them?

MM: I have structures in various places. The Movement Café panels are in my studio, the scaffolding and shipping containers went to a project Cathedral are doing in Brighton. The Discovery Pavilion is in storage in Birmingham and the Temple of Agape is in storage in Bermondsey. Scaffolding was hired that time, so that went back. As much as I can control things I really don't want to make things that then get thrown away. They all can have another use. I am working on a project in Finsbury Park and I would love to be able to make a new pavilion in the park using all these reclaimed panels. If I don't do it there, I will do it somewhere soon I hope.

How did the Pavilion in Birmingham (2013) project come about? How did you engage people in that case?

MM: I had worked on two exhibitions at the Birmingham Museum. One was Home of Metal with Lisa Meyer from Capsule, the events creators. They had been given the task of producing a three month Discovery Season for the opening of the new Library. Lisa had seen the temporary installation I had been doing and wanted me to do one for the Discovery Season, as a focus point for the festival. It was to be a place for events, that could be transformed depending on who was occupying it. Our aim for the Pavilion and the season was to connect people with the new Library, so they could see that it was there for them and look at libraries with a fresh eye and mind. The neon crown of signs was originated from discussions with the Birmingham 2022 group.

FIGURE 6.18: above / the interior of The Deptford Project featured furniture hand-painted by Morag Myerscough and Luke Morgan

FIGURE 6.19: above / signs on top of The Movement Cafe spell out tweets by Olympic Poet Lemn Sissay

FIGURE 6.20: above top / built in two weeks, The Pavilion was hand-painted with symbols used in online communication
FIGURE 6.21: above bottom / the Pavilion hosted an 18-week programme of creative residencies with artists and filmakers

Where does your love of colour come from?

A very talked about subject at the moment! My mother is a textile artist and we always had loads of colour around the house. We would go with her to buy fabrics and she would dye wools at home with vegetables and berries, so I was exposed to the subtlety of colour from a very early age and it must have just got embedded in me. When I was at Central Saint Martins I was dismayed when the only colours people thought existed were primaries. It made me react quite strongly – I never wanted to be restricted like that. Colour is amazing but has to be used carefully; it's much more dependent on surrounding conditions than people think. One of my favourite backdrops is concrete.

Do you see your projects as art or architecture? How do you think you fit into the temporary architecture world?

Gosh, this is a hard one. I would prefer not to be defined. I have not tried to do architecture or art; I'm just making work. I like the idea that the formal labels defined by education can be blurred. I think I will leave it for others to categorise my work rather than me. I want to make places that people connect to, enjoy and get involved in. The subject of my talks is 'Belonging' and I always start my talk with this Chinese proverb – 'Make happy those who are near and those who are far will come.'

FIGURE 6.22: above / the plywood panels and hand-painted signs of the Temple of Agape were supported by a scaffolding structure

PERSPECTIVE /
LEARNING FROM CANNING TOWN CARAVANSERAI: A TEMPORARY TOWN AND ITS LEGACY

CANY ASH

In 2011, Ash Sakula Architects, together with EXYZT, Just Make Tea, The Kindest, Technology Will Save Us, Dougald Hine, Wayward Plants and Sara Muzio, won the Meanwhile London competition to occupy a site opposite Canning Town Station with a temporary, pop-up project of five years' duration.

Our aim was to create a new kind of public space for London, for hosting businesses, workshops, conversations and events, all run in an environment that valued experimentation and creativity in the context of community.

THIS IS TEMPORARY

It would be a space with opportunities to trial small businesses in micro-enterprise kiosks, and there would be a community garden for local growers, a playground for children and a stage for local performance groups and events. And it would be a laboratory for building in a different sort of way, using whatever materials we could beg, steal or borrow.

Every aspect of the project was subject to intense debate during the competition phase, including the name, Canning Town Caravanserai. The ancient trading posts along the Silk Road – 'glocal' places of cultural exchange and wealth generation – suggested a robust precedent for the commercial and social mixing we wanted to pursue in our project. We liked the five-year time span – much longer than most pop-ups. We wanted to see how incremental development within a temporary project could mimic the conditions of how cities actually evolve over time.

In mid-recession 2011, money was scarce, and the project was short of the funding needed to kickstart it properly. Other team members decided to put their energies into other, more tangible projects, leaving us at Ash Sakula with the task of making the Caravanserai a reality with these very limited resources.

We went on to build a small but impressive town of structures, which constitutes an alternative reality for many of its fans in Canning Town and further afield. Creating the legal space for experimentation was hard work – we were given exactly the same tasks and hurdles to jump as regular developers – but the project has had many successes, as well as a few setbacks.

To stimulate ideas, source new designs and recruit commercial energy we held a series of competitions. The Dragon's Kiosk in 2012 was a two-stage pitching challenge to occupy the Caravanserai's trading kiosks. Flitched, in 2013, took its inspiration from flitched beams, where steel strengthens timber, timber stabilises steel. We gave contestants a specific menu of scavenged and donated materials and a requirement that architects and engineers work together, and set them the task of covering the largest possible area for a winter workshop and rainproof performance arena.

Currently, we are coming to the end of our occupation. At the end of 2015, the site will be cleared for the next phase of development of Canning Town's new commercial centre. The Caravanserai, now a registered charity, needs to consider what it has achieved and learnt from Canning Town.

Firstly, the openness provided by intensely friendly hosting and the permeability of any ideas or energy offered by visitors was all-important to the ethos of the project. In building a structure or creating an event, there's always a balance to be struck between being impressive enough to attract attention and visitors, and the kind of improvisation and roughness which invites participation. This led to a scenography of crude exoticism, so the site was entered through Turkish Delight-inspired portals, the theatre had a 'flying carpet' canopy, there was a palm tree built from scrap materials. The enclosing walls and relative order of the Caravanserai makes a place for sane, convivial activities, in contrast to the post-Olympic construction fever and the endless empty ski lift capsules crossing the sky. In this ordered, temporary world we created four 'guilds' –Trading, Making, Growing and Performing – each with their own hashtags and specific structures on the site.

Another aspect of making which we hope may inform the post-Caravanserai development of this terrain is that our small constructions are often laden with place-enriching anecdotes, such as the making of Roberto's quadruple see-saw, Derek's café sign, Amy's triangular tree planters, Amara's clever up-and-down chairs, and Iliona's self-firing brick dome.

We have also been exploring how we could salvage some of the energy and resources we have built so painstakingly. Another competition we set up in 2014, Parks on Wheels – part of the GLA's Pocket Parks programme – explored ways of making mobile parks which could be moved from one site to another. We had in mind exploring how community energy could wittily be conserved and moved between interim sites.

Ultimately, the Caranvanserai's legacy is the example it sets and the confidence it gives others to make use of slack space and do more 'tryouts' in the city. During its time, the Caravanserai has hosted delegations from all parts. They included a delegation from the Mayor of Seoul in South Korea, who spent a day at the Caravanserai looking at how to make more village settings and networks in the city, and a delegation of landscape architects from Norway who want to investigate innovative ways of creating social spaces within parks. We hope its example will continue to inspire. Already it has featured in a Brazilian book on incremental urbanism, and in podcasts by Labkultur.TV from the Ruhr in Germany, and by the Londonist.

All in all, we hope the closure of the Caravanserai this autumn will be the end of a chapter, but not of the story. We look forward to seeing other experiments in temporary city-making in London and elsewhere, where a genuine enthusiasm, agility and genius for improvisation can keep us skipping one step ahead of the bulldozers in creating places, albeit fleeting ones, where sane societal values can flourish.

CONCLUSION /
CATE ST HILL

For years now, the word pop-up has been bandied about, implying a circus of tricks used to advertise and popularise, to provoke spectacle and pageantry, to create an immediate, photo-ready frenzy. In its simplest form, temporary architecture can be trite, quick and cheaply put together – but this book has shown that there is a group of imaginative, original, young architects and designers who are creating more intuitive gestures in the built environment, backed up by rigorous research, community engagement and much deeper social ambitions. They're making studied responses to contemporary lifestyles and changing cityscapes, and in the process they're causing a subtle but profound shift within the architecture profession. Alternative modes of practising architecture are invariably emerging from temporary architecture, ranging from multidisciplinary, research-based design to collaborative, participative building and self-initiated, self-built projects. In these cases, the role of the architect is expanding to include storyteller, historian, urban planner, psychologist, facilitator and communicator. Collaborations are further blurring these boundaries. Neither is it always necessary to go through the traditional rigmarole of architectural education any more.

One concern highlighted in the book is what happens to the materials of these structures once their temporary existence has ended. Some architects had designed projects to be dismountable and reusable; some had components still dotted around their studios and back gardens waiting for the next opportunity; others didn't know what had happened to their structures at all. 'What I think is a bit of a shame with temporary architecture is that there's no recycling process,' notes Aberrant Architecture's Kevin Haley. 'At the end of Clerkenwell Design Week, if we had said no, we didn't want the Tiny Travelling Theatre, they were literally just going to bin it.' While across the world there are grass-roots online platforms such as Freecycle that allow people to give (and get) domestic paraphernalia for free, perhaps in today's throwaway society there should also be a similar initiative for discarded material, not just from temporary architecture, but from exhibitions, arts fairs, theatre sets, music festivals and so on – something that Folke Köbberling and Martin Kaltwasser tried (unfortunately unsuccessfully) to do in 2008. For the most part, though, the architects and designers here didn't see their projects as wasteful throwaway objects, but meaningful investments into a space or into the development of longer-term ideas.

Also looking past the impermanence of these projects, another fundamental question that came up time and time again throughout the interviews was that of what we define as temporary. How long is temporary? Is it five minutes, six months, a year? Or could it be 20 years, even 100 years? Many of the projects included in this book have indeed stayed in place far longer than their initial time frame proposed. Morag Myerscough's Movement Café was meant to be in Greenwich three months but lasted a year; Studio Weave's Paleys upon Pilers had planning permission for six months, but stayed for two years; Folke Köbberling and Martin Kaltwasser's Amphis for Wysing Arts Centre in Cambridgeshire was likewise supposed to be around for two years, but has stayed for eight; Practice Architecture's Frank's Cafe has reappeared each summer since 2009; and EXYZT has returned to the same vacant site in Southwark three times over a period of seven years. Meantime, Aberrant Architecture is working on a public arts commission in Swansea that is purportedly permanent, but will only be there for 20 years. Similarly Studio Weave's Lullaby Factory at Great Ormond Street Hospital in London will be in position for 15 years.

In fact, many buildings in our cities that were meant to be short-lived have stayed – the Eiffel Tower in Paris, the London Eye and the Millennium Dome in London, and the postwar prefabs from south London to Newport, Wales, to pick just a few examples. The Serpentine Pavilions are sold after each summer turn, and have been transformed into beachside restaurants, private garden follies and a theme park marquee. Many of these constructions (in our public spaces) would probably not have been approved if they had been permanent from the outset: people are wary of anything new that might make mistakes and blight our cities – but once we get used to something, we become attached to it and hate to see it disappear. As Studio Weave's Eddie Blake suggests in Chapter 3, 'That's to do with people thinking they're going to hedge their bets and just say it's temporary – they get to like it and it's actually a scary decision to say, "This is going to last a hundred years."'

Perhaps it's time to rethink the dividing line between temporary and permanence. Perhaps it doesn't need to be so prescriptive and portioned off into categories. 'Short-life projects can be a great way to test an idea that can then grow in strength, demonstrate itself, and potentially evolve into something more permanent,' says Practice Architecture in Chapter 4. 'Over the years, our ideas about what the space of impermanence means have gone through quite a shift. We have an increasing desire to make things that are solid, embedded, invested – that have longevity and that represent an investment in and expression of a geographical community.' Indeed, just because temporary architecture is only around for a short time, that doesn't mean that it can't be as considered as something more longer-term. The projects shown here have the ability to catalyse subtler and wider-ranging effects, as shown for instance by The Decorators' project for Chrisp Street Market. That scheme, which involved setting up a 'Town Team' to meet regularly, as well as more tangible changes such as new market furniture, has gone on to act as a pilot for two other attention-starved London markets in need of rejuvenation.

As the projects in this book illustrate, temporary architecture can do all the things permanent 'bricks and mortar' architecture can do, and more besides: it can test new technologies and materials, it can be innovative and experimental, it can be sustainable, reusable and recyclable, it can enrich and engage communities, and it can help foster a sense of place. And all of this without the risk and constraints of permanence: if it's a mistake or doesn't work, then just dismantle it and think again. It's not that much different from the demolition of the 1960s and 1970s Brutalist monoliths, 10, 20,

50 years after their construction. In this way, temporary architecture may not seem like a waste of resources at all.

The interviews in this book have also shown how the process of temporary architecture is essentially no different to that of a permanent project. For these architects and designers, temporary projects involve the same design processes, the same ideas about architecture and the city, the same aesthetic concerns, the same social and political issues, just in a more condensed form. 'If you let go of the exclusive emphasis on structure and think about what was produced as a way of working, a set of relationships, a demonstration of possibility, the temporariness starts to look more background,' notes Assemble. Yet, temporary architecture has much to teach permanent architecture about breaking the rules slightly, thinking outside the box and making our built environment accessible, open, intuitive, unrestrictive and that little bit playful. These should be standards for every project. Much of the work here is inherently democratic, with communities and volunteers invited to take part in their conception and thus reconnecting us to the process by which our urban spaces are made. With temporary architecture, as EXYZT says, 'everybody can be the architects of our world'.

ENDNOTES

1. Beatriz Colomina 'Unbreathed Air', in Dirk Van Den Heuvel and Max Risselada (eds.), Alison and Peter Smithson: From the House of the Future to a House of Today (Rotterdam: 010 Publishing, 2004), p.33.

2. Peter Smithson, 'Staging the Possible', in Alison and Peter Smithson, Italian Thoughts (London, 1993), p.16. Quoted in Van Heuvel and Riselada 2004.

3. Sam Jacob, Make it real. Architecture as enactment (Moscow: Strelka Press, 2012). Kindle Edition.

4. The Dalston Mill, commissioned by the Barbican Centre in the context of the exhibition Radical Nature – Art and Architecture for a Changing Planet 1969-2009, was an installation that lasted three weeks in 2009. A disused railway in Dalston, East London was transformed into a fully functioning flour mill with a community kitchen and bakery oven all open to the public. The project also included a wheat field, a recreation of artist Agnes Denes's Wheatfield – A Confrontation, originally planted in New York in 1982. The project comprised a public programme of events organised in collaboration with local structures such as Arcola Academy, baking and cooking classes, urban sustainability talks, workshops, artist talks and a bike-powered cinema hosted by Magnificent Revolution. Its construction was developed through apprenticeship schemes.

5. Architectural fictions are usually identified in drawings, photomontages, texts or other mediums excluding the building. See, for example, Pedro Gadanho and Susana Oliveira, Introduction, in Once Upon a Place: Architecture and Fiction (Lisbon: Caldeidoscópio, 2013), pp.7-8; David Glissen, 'Architecture Fiction: a short review of a young concept', HTC Experiments (22 Feb. 2009), accessed 20 Nov. 2014: http://htcexperiments.org/2009/02/22/architecture-fiction-—-a-short-review-of-a-young-concept; Bruce Sterling, 'Architects of the Near Future', Wired (31 Dec. 2008), accessed 20 Nov. 2014: http://bldgblog.blogspot.com/2008/12/architects-of-near-future.html.

6. Marie-Laure Ryan, 'Possible Worlds and Accessibility Relations: A Semantic Typology of Fiction' in Poetics Today, vol.12, no.3 (Autumn 1991), pp.553-76.

7. Doreen Maitre, Literature and Possible Worlds (London: Middlesex Polytechnic Press, 1983).

8. Arjun Appadurai, The Future as a Cultural Fact (London: Verso, 2014).

INDEX

IMAGE CREDITS

Aberrant Architecture — 73, 74, 76, 83
Andy Matthews — 104 (left), 126
Assemble — 106, 108, 115
Atelier ChanChan — 57
BarkowPhoto, courtesy of The Living — 16, 18
Ben Quinton — 80
Brice Pelleschi — 119, 125 (bottom)
Camilla Mantovani — 149, 173
Charles Roussel, courtesy of The Living — 8
Cristobal Palma — 6, 24, 27-29
David Vintiner — 113
DOSFOTOS — 36, 40, 53, 56 (top), 58-59, 61 (bottom)
EXYZT — 102, 117-118, 122-123, 125 (top)
Gareth Gardner — 176, 181-182, 196, 201-203
Gruppe — 178, 190 (left & right), 192-195
Guglielmo Rossi — 39
GUN Architects — 35 (top & bottom)
Heather McDonough — 62-63
IED Madrid — 167
Iwan Baan, courtesy of The Living — 14, 23
Jakob Spriestersbach — 42, 46
Jan Gregor Köbberling — 153
Jim Stephenson — 43, 51 (bottom), 93-94
John Sturrock — 184, 188
Julie Guiches — 116
Justin Lui, courtesy of The Living — 22
Köbberling/Kaltwasser — 146-147, 152, 154-156, 158-165
Lewis Jones/Assemble — 112
Luke Morgan — 197
Maddison Graphic — 48 (top & bottom)
Marco Canevacci — 144, 148, 166, 169-171, 172 (top), 174-175
Max Creasy — 51 (top left)
Mike Massaro — 127
Morley von Sternberg — 110
Oskar Proctor — 131-137, 139
Philipp Ebeling — 61 (top)
Practice Architecture — 100, 104 (right), 129-130
Richard Wentworth with Gruppe — 179, 187, 189
Simon Kennedy — 78-79, 84-85
Simone Serlenga — 172
Studio Weave — 68, 70, 72, 86-92, 96-99
Sue Barr/Architectural Association — 32, 34
Supergrouplondon — 199-200
The Decorators — 52, 55, 56 (bottom)
The Living — 15, 17, 19-21
Valerie Bennett/Architectural Association — 10, 25, 30-31
Valerie Bennett/British Council 2012 — 77
We Made That — 45, 47, 51 (top right)
We Made That & Wolfram Wiedner — 49